NOW YOU KNOW
KNOW

THE BIBLE

T0094622

NOW YOU KNOW

KNOW

THE BIBLE

Doug Lennox

DUNDURN PRESS
TORONTO

Project Editor: Michael Carroll
Editor: Patricia Kennedy
Copy Editor: Matt Baker
Design: Jesse Hooper
Printer: Webcom

Library and Archives Canada Cataloguing in Publication

Lennox, Doug
   Now you know the Bible / by Doug Lennox.

Issued also in an electronic format.
ISBN 978-1-55488-798-9

   1. Bible--Miscellanea. I. Title.

BS538.L45 2010   220   C2010-902438-9

1   2   3   4   5   14   13   12   11   10

We acknowledge the support of the **Canada Council for the Arts** and the **Ontario Arts Council** for our publishing program. We also acknowledge the financial support of the **Government of Canada** through the **Canada Book Fund** and **The Association for the Export of Canadian Books**, and the **Government of Ontario** through the **Ontario Book Publishers Tax Credit program**, and the **Ontario Media Development Corporation**.

Care has been taken to trace the ownership of copyright material used in this book. The author and the publisher welcome any information enabling them to rectify any references or credits in subsequent editions.

J. Kirk Howard, President

Printed and bound in Canada.
www.dundurn.com

Dundurn Press	Gazelle Book Services Limited	Dundurn Press
3 Church Street, Suite 500	White Cross Mills	2250 Military Road
Toronto, Ontario, Canada	High Town, Lancaster, England	Tonawanda, NY
M5E 1M2	LA1 4XS	U.S.A. 14150

contents

Preface 9

The Book 13

The Old Testament

The Beginning: Genesis 27

The Books of Moses: Exodus, Leviticus,
Numbers, Deuteronomy 40

Getting Settled: The Books of Samuel,
Kings, and Chronicles 55

Judges and Priests: Joshua, Judges, and Ruth 71

The Prophets, Major and Minor 80

Exile and Homecoming: Ezra, Nehemiah,
Esther, and Daniel 89

Writings, Poetry, and Songs: Job, Psalms,
Proverbs, Ecclesiastes, Song of Songs 97

The New Testament

The Life of Jesus: Matthew Mark, Luke, and John 109

The Early Church: Acts, Romans, Letters to the
Churches, Revelation 149

The Bible and Culture 162

Question and Feature List 175

preface

The first thing to be said is that this is a work of entertainment. Although I certainly acknowledge the central place the Bible has in the lives of many believers, and the reverence with which it is held, this book does not attempt to address the deeper ideas that shape the faith of so many.

What these pages contain are the interesting facts, amusing details, and cultural influences that swirl around the ancient volume.

Because the Bible has so long and so profound a cultural history, this is not an easy task. It has been around, in some form or other, for over two thousand years and has informed Western culture for a good part of that time. Prior to the twentieth century, most people in the Western world, regardless of their beliefs, would have been familiar with the stories and the symbols of the Bible. In art, for instance, biblical and Classical subject matter was almost all artists painted — if they wanted acceptance. With the exception of the genre painting by artists such as

Vermeer and Van Eyck and the portraits of the wealthy and powerful, it is hard to find anything *other* than religious or classical depictions prior to the nineteenth century, as you may have noticed in a stroll through any art gallery. While subject matter in literature roamed more widely, religious allusions were still everywhere.

It is almost impossible to study the history of Western art or literature without knowing something about the Bible.

Obviously, the problem with a book such as this is not lack of material but too much material. I admit freely, then, that the choices of what to discuss are totally individual — dare I say eccentric — and are not consciously weighted in any way.

As an organizing principle, I've followed the Bible itself and divided the book into Old Testament and New Testament sections. Within those sections, the chapters follow, for the most part, the order of the books of the Bible. An exception would be the grouping of the books of Ezra, Esther, Nehemiah, and Daniel into a chapter dealing with the captivity of the Israelites in Babylon and their return to Israel. The books all deal with a similar period but don't fall together in the Bible. Another exception is the grouping of the wisdom literature and poetry of the Old Testament. In this, the book follows the organization of the *The Bible for Dummies*, which is excellent (yes, really).

The Old Testament section moves from the story of Adam and Eve through Noah and the flood, to the flight of the Israelites from Egypt under the leadership of Moses. Then comes the settling of the Israelites in the Promised Land, the establishment of a priesthood and the anointing of a king, the rules of David and his son Solomon, the warnings of the prophets, the captivity of the Jews and their exile in Babylon, and the return to Israel. The final chapter looks at the amazing collections of poetry and wise saying collected in Psalms, Proverbs, Ecclesiastes, and Song of Songs/Solomon — oh yes, and in Job, which deals with that eternal question, "Why do bad things happen to good people?"

The New Testament section starts with the four gospels (find out what *gospel* means) that recount the life and works of Jesus, moves on to the story of the missionary work of the apostles and the founding of the early church, and ends with that head-scratcher, Revelation.

Don't expect any illumination on weighty subjects. This is the book that will ask such questions as:

- "What was the fruit that Adam and Eve ate in the Garden of Eden?"

- "How big was the Ark?"

- "Who was only left-handed person mentioned in the Bible?"

- "Who were the wise men anyway?"

- "Did John the Baptist found the Baptist church?"

- "What happened to the twelve apostles?"

We will also look at the way the Bible has become part of our language. Any book that plays such a large role in history and culture will inevitably enter the language, both in specific words and in expressions. We will examine the biblical roots of such words as *scapegoat, maudlin,* and *petrel,* and the names of holidays such as Easter, but particularly striking are the number of expressions and sayings that we use every day, sometimes without being aware that they come from the Bible. Some examples are:

- "At one's wits' end"

- "By the skin of your teeth"

- "Eat, drink, and be merry"

- "A fly in the ointment"

- "No rest for the wicked"

- "The apple of your eye"

Then there are all those ways that the Bible informs culture. Here are works of art, books, movies, and songs (particularly spirituals and hymns) that draw on the Bible for inspiration, or simply use biblical phrases and names to link the work to deeper themes, as with Herman Melville's *Moby-Dick*. Sure, it's about whaling, but it's also about false gods and the destructive choices one makes.

Needless to say, in this area, we can only scrape the surface.

With the deepest of respect to the Jewish reader — and to the Catholic and Eastern Orthodox readers as well — the Bible that has been referred to throughout is the King James Bible. The Hebrew Bible and the Apocrypha are touched on, but I've chosen not to cover them in detail, in case the subject balloons out of control.

Although its language is not the language of today, I have also chosen to quote from the King James Bible, because its influence has been so all-pervasive. Admittedly, there have been countless fine translations done since the advent of the King James Bible in 1611, but many of the phrases I will discuss and the references to other works that will pop up reflect the wording of the good old KJV (King James Version). I will also use the traditional method of citing chapters and verses: the chapter first, followed by a colon and then the verse. For example, John 3:16 refers to the third chapter of the book of John, and the sixteenth verse. I will also use the dating designations B.C.E. (before the common era) and C.E. (common era). The years are exactly the same as they would be if B.C. and A.D. were used.

My heartfelt thanks to the many scholars who have done the heavy lifting. They are the ones who can tell us the meaning of phrases and words in translation, who can explain the customs of the ancient world, and who can explain whether the evidence backs up a particular reading of the text — and when it come to the Bible, there are as many multiplied errors, crackpot interpretations, and conspiracy agendas as there are words in the Bible itself. With the help of these scholars and their work, I hope I have avoided passing on any of these more *original* theories. The facts are interesting enough!

the Book

What does the name *Bible* mean?

You're probably used to talking about the "books" of the Bible. This is a clue to the origin of its name, because the Bible is not really one book but a collection of books or writings by a number of authors, which were brought together much later to form the Bible we know. Because the *Bible* is a library, its name comes from *ta biblia*, which is Greek for "the books" or "the scrolls."

What is the Hebrew Bible?

This refers to the books of the Hebrew Scriptures, which are the same books that make up the Old Testament in the Christian Bible, and which were almost all written originally in Hebrew. In the Hebrew Bible, however, a number of the books are in a different order than they are in the Christian tradition.

The first five books of scripture — Genesis, Exodus, Leviticus, Numbers, and Deuteronomy — make up the books of the the *Torah*, from a Hebrew word for "law." These same books are also called the *Pentateuch*, from the Greek for "five scrolls."

Who first collected the books of the Old Testament?

When the Babylonians destroyed Jerusalem in 586 B.C.E., they carried many of the people off to Babylon, levelled the palace and temple in Jerusalem, and destroyed a rich library of recorded material — a popular pastime among conquerors. What remained of the writings, however, were saved and taken to Babylon by the captives. The Israelites struggled to keep their culture alive in exile, and a project was mounted to pull the material together and edit it. The priest Ezra has been credited with organizing this effort and carrying the scrolls back to Jerusalem when it was rebuilt.

When was the Bible first translated?

The Old Testament was first translated from Hebrew into Greek around 250 B.C.E. By this time, Alexander the Great had rampaged over much of the known world, spreading Greek culture far and wide. Because of this, fewer Jews were able to read Hebrew, and a Greek translation was prepared. It was known as the *Septuagint*, Greek for "seventy," because of the belief that seventy scribes independently produced identical translations of the Torah.

How many passages do some claim were written by God?

Because the Bible says some thirty-eight hundred times that "God said" or "thus says the Lord," there are those who believe these passages were written by God. Ditto for the Ten Commandments.

How many versions of the Bible are there in English?

This sort of question is almost impossible to answer definitively, but it has been estimated that there have been over 450 versions.

When was the Bible first translated into English?

The first translation of the whole Bible into English (from Latin) was done by John Wycliffe (et al.) in the late fourteenth century. The Church was very opposed to this, fearing that those who weren't specially trained might misunderstand the text once they got their hands on it. John Wycliffe managed to die a natural death, but soon after, his bones were dug up and burned for heresy.

This must have given others something to think about, because it wasn't until approximately 150 years later, in 1526, that William

Tyndale made the New Testament available. Tyndale wasn't as lucky as Wycliffe. In 1536, in Antwerp, he was strangled at the stake and then his body was burned.

In 1535, Miles Coverdale produced the first complete Bible to be printed in English, translating from Latin, Wycliffe's English, and Martin Luther's German.

History doesn't record what Coverdale thought when he heard about Tyndale's fate, but when Tyndale's friend John Rogers brought out another translation in 1537, he was shaken enough to call it the Thomas Matthew Bible. Quick thinking, John.

Nonetheless, it seems the tide had turned. In 1539, when Coverdale revised the Matthew Bible to produce the Great Bible, it became the first authorized Bible printed in English. King Henry VIII, no less, ordered that it be put in every church.

Which Bible did Shakespeare use?

Quickies
Did you know ...
• that the second edition of the Geneva Bible reads, "blessed are the placemakers," instead of "blessed are the peacemakers."

After King Henry VIII and his sickly son Edward VI had died, his eldest daughter, Mary Tudor, came to the throne. Although her father had broken with Rome to found the English church, Mary remained a staunch Roman Catholic, and she lost no time in persecuting Protestants in England, earning her the nickname "Bloody Mary."

Some of the Protestants who fled England during her reign ended up in Geneva, where, in 1560, they produced the Geneva Bible, a revision of the English Bible. (Interestingly, Mary was already dead by this time, and had been succeeded by her Protestant half-sister, Elizabeth.)

The Geneva Bible is significant for several reasons.

It is the first edition of the Bible in which the now-familiar numbered verses appear. The New Testament, according to legend, was first divided into chapters and verses in 1544 by a printer named R. Stephens.

When the early pilgrim fathers (and mothers) stepped ashore in the New World in the 1620s, it was the Geneva Bible they were carrying. Although the King James Bible had been published by then, it was a production of the monarchy and the official English church, with which they were at odds.

This was also the Bible that was used and quoted by Shakespeare, along with Coverdale's Great Bible.

When was the King James Bible published?

King James I succeeded Elizabeth I on her death in 1603. Not wasting any time, in 1604 he issued a command for the production of a new translation of the Bible. Fifty-four scholars worked from Greek and Hebrew

The Books of the Bible
(As found in the King James Version)

Old Testament		The New Testament	
• Genesis	• Ecclesiastes	• Matthew	• Philemon
• Exodus	• Song of	• Mark	• Hebrews
• Leviticus	Solomon	• Luke	(Epistle to the
• Numbers	• Isaiah	• John	Hebrews)
• Deuteronomy	• Jeremiah	• Acts (the Acts of	• James (Epistle
• Joshua	• Lamentations	the Apostles)	of James)
• Judges	• Ezekiel	• Romans (the	• I Peter
• Ruth	• Daniel	Epistle to the	• II Peter
• I Samuel	• Hosea	Romans)	• I John
• II Samuel	• Joel	• I Corinthians	• II John
• I Kings	• Amos	• II Corinthians	• III John
• II Kings	• Obadiah	• Galatians	• Jude
• I Chronicles	• Jonah	• Ephesians	• Revelation
• II Chronicles	• Micah	• Philippians	
• Ezra	• Nahum	• Colossians	
• Nehemiah	• Habakkuk	• I Thessalonians	
• Esther	• Zephaniah	• II Thessalonians	
• Job	• Haggai	• I Timothy	
• Psalms	• Zechariah	• II Timothy	
• Proverbs	• Malachi	• Titus	

Catholic and Eastern Orthodox Bibles include the Apocrypha.

manuscripts and English editions, and they completed the Bible by 1611. It blends scholarship and poetry in a version of the Bible that is still widely loved, although countless translations have followed.

What is the Apocrypha?

Many who are familiar with the King James Bible and other Protestant versions will not know the Apocrypha. That is because it appears only in Catholic and Eastern Orthodox versions, not in the Protestant Bible or in the Hebrew Bible.

Between the times the Greek and Latin translations of Hebrew scriptures were done, Jewish scholars decided that some of the books included in the Hebrew Bible were, though important, not divinely inspired and should not be included. When Saint Jerome translated the Greek translation (Septuagint) into Latin (Vulgate), he agreed with the decision, but there was much disagreement. As a result, they weren't removed until the Protestant Reformation, and appear in the Catholic and Eastern Orthodox versions, where they are placed at the end of the Old Testament.

This explains the name: *Apocrypha* means "hidden" in Greek.

How many books are there in the Protestant Bible?

There are sixty-six books, thirty-nine in the Old Testament and twenty-seven in the New Testament.

Quickies
Did you know ...
- that the Bible is the most shoplifted book in the world, while approximately fifty Bibles are sold every minute. Presumably those who aren't buying their Bibles are shoplifting. Perhaps they should read the Ten Commandments first.

What did Voltaire get wrong?

The French Enlightenment writer and philosopher Voltaire (1694–1778) said that, within a hundred years of his day, Christianity would pass into the obscurity of history.

Ironically, within fifty years of his death, the Geneva Bible Society was using Voltaire's house and printing press to produce Bibles.

How many Bibles are distributed in the United States every day?

According to statistics given out by the Gideons, the International Bible Society, and others, there are about 128,000 Bibles distributed every day.

What is *bibliomancy*?

Bibliomancy is the word for the use of books in divination. The book used is usually a sacred book, and for Christians the Bible is most commonly used.

To determine the will of God or to gain guidance for some action, people close their eyes, let the chosen book fall open at random, open their eyes, and hope to be guided by the first words they see.

In early Christianity, the believers would sometimes pay special attention to whatever was being sung as they entered the church. The more formal method however, was to open the scriptures and read the first thing they saw. This was called the *Sortes Sacrae*, or the "Holy Lots."

The Apocrypha

Even though the Apocrypha does not appear in the Hebrew Bible, the material it contains deals with many stories of great importance in Hebrew tradition, such as the Maccabee Rebellion.

It is also important to students of art history, since a number of works of art represent, or allude to, material taken from the Apocrypha. One popular subject was the story of Susanna and the Elders, in which a virtuous woman was spied on by elders of the church as she bathed. This gave artists the chance to paint a luscious nude while sticking to a biblical theme.

The books of the Apocrypha
• Tobit
• Judith
• Additions to Esther
• Wisdom of Solomon
• Ecclesiasticus
• Baruch
• Letter of Jeremiah
• Prayer of Azariah and the Song of the Three Jews
• Susanna
• Bel and the Dragon
• I Maccabee
• II Maccabee
• I Edras
• II Edras
• Prayer of Manasseh

To these, the Eastern Orthodox church adds:
• III Macabees
• IV Macabees
• Psalm 151

Although most Christian groups disapprove of divination, somehow this method has survived, though it has no official sanction.

While it has nothing to do with sacred texts, another method is to choose a book and passage at random. That is how poet Robert Browning found himself consulting *Cerutti's Italian Grammar* for guidance in his courtship of fellow poet Elizabeth Barrett.

Bible Stats

- Number of chapters in the Bible: 1,189. (929 in the Old Testament, and 260 in the New Testament)
- Number of verses in the Bible: 31,173 (23,214 in the OT, and 7,959 in the NT)
- Number of words in the Bible: 774,746 (593,493 in the OT, and 181,253 in the NT)
- Longest verse: Esther 8:9, with 78 words
- Shortest verse: John 11:35, with two words
- Shortest book (by number of words): III John
- Longest book: Psalms, with 150 chapters
- Longest chapter: Psalms 119, with 176 verses

It is estimated that the Bible should take seventy hours to read, though when the American Foundation for the Blind recorded the entire King James Version in 1944, it took eighty-four and a half hours. Slow readers?

What was the first major book printed with movable type?

The Gutenberg Bible, also called the 42-Line Bible or the Mazarin Bible, is an edition of the Latin text and was printed in 1454–55. Its appearance marked a revolution in printing history: the beginning of the era of the printed book, which is referred to as the Gutenberg Revolution.

This Bible is the result of much experimentation on the part of Johannes Gutenberg. During the printing he had to develop a new kind of oil-based ink that would stick to the metal type, and his efforts to print in two colours had to be suspended. The red detailing was continued by hand.

It is thought about 180 copies were printed, of which 135 were on paper and 45 were on vellum. As of 2009, only 48 copies were thought to exist. The last complete copy sold in 1978 for $2.2 million.

What is the most expensive modern Bible?

In 1998, St. John's Abbey and University in Minnesota decided to pay tribute to an ancient Benedictine tradition by commissioning calligrapher Donald Jackson to produce a hand-written and hand-illuminated Bible. The final result, named the St. John's Bible, is a work of art that is written on vellum using hand-ground pigments and inks.

On the completion of the St. John's Bible, the College began producing a 360-copy Heritage Edition. While the original Bible is not for sale, a copy of the Heritage Edition sells for $130,000.

What is the largest printed Bible?

In 1928, Louis Waynai of Los Angeles began to print the entire King James Bible using a large rubber-stamp press that he had made. When he finished the job two years later, he had produced the world's largest Bible, measuring nearly four feet tall (43.5 inches), and over eight feet (98 inches) across when the book is open. When the book is closed, the spine is almost three feet (98 inches) thick. It has 8,048 pages and weighs 1,094 pounds.

In 1956, the Waynai Bible was donated to Abilene Christian College, where it is still on display.

Some claim the title of largest Bible belongs to the Macklin Bible of 1800, which was printed in seven volumes. However, each volume is a mere two feet high and 130 pounds, falling far short of the sheer mass of the Waynai Bible. It may, however, be the largest Bible to be mass-produced using a printing press.

What is the world's smallest Bible?

In 1901, David Bryce and Company, Glasgow, produced a tiny Bible, known at the time as the "mini mite" or "thumb Bible." Just about one inch wide and less than half an inch thick, it could sit in the bowl of a spoon. It came in a case with metal hinges and included a magnifying glass to help the reader make out the type.

The Bryce Bible was not an eccentric production at the time. It was printed at a time of new developments in lithography and photo reduction, and typesetters were trying out the technology by creating a number of tiny books. The nineteenth century was seen as a pinnacle of achievement for the production of miniature books.

In 2007, the Bryce Bible was in the news again when renovators working on a cottage in Ewerby, Lincolnshire, made a discovery in the chimney. Stuffed in the brickwork was a child's boot, and inside the boot was a copy of the Bryce Bible, still encased in fragments of the hinged case.

According to local antiquities experts, this was probably intended to ward off evil. The use of shoes as a sort of spirit trap dates back to the fourteenth century, and lingered on long after people lost track of the history.

Bibles with Errors

Yes, typos happen — and so do questionable translations. There are Bibles out there that are named after the amusing or head-scratching irregularities that made them famous. Some of the best known, in a very long list, are:

- **The Bug Bible:** The 1535 Bible produced by Myles Coverdale translates as "bugge" what the KJV translates as "terror." Therefore Psalm 91:5 reads, "Thou shalt not be affrayed for any bugges by night." Tell it to a camper. In fairness to Myles, in his day *bugge* meant "spectre" or "ghost."
- **The Treacle Bible:** Also known as Beck's Bible. This 1549 edition of the Great Bible translated as "treacle" what modern translations translate as "balm." Jeremiah 8:22 therefore reads "Is there no treacle in Gilead?"
- **The Placemaker's Bible:** In addition to the typo for "peacemakers" that gave the second edition of the Geneva Bible (1562) its nickname, the heading for Luke 21 reads, "Christ condemneth the poor widow." That's "commendeth" when they get it right.
- **The Breeches Bible:** In this 1579 edition of the KJV, Adam and Eve make themselves "breeches." The more acceptable translation is "coverings."
- **The Wicked Bible/Sinner's Bible/Adulterer's Bible:** This 1631 edition of the KJV positively commands people to commit adultery.
- **The Unrighteous Bible:** A missing "not" in this 1653 KJV makes I Corinthians 6:9 read, "Know ye not that the unrighteous shall inherit the kingdom of God?"
- **The Sin On Bible:** In this 1716 edition of the KJV, John 8:11 reads "Go and sin on more."
- **The Vinegar Bible:** Instead of the Parable of the Vineyard, this 1717 edition of the KJV announces the Parable of the Vinegar.
- **The Rebecca's Camels Bible:** In one place in this 1823 edition, the word *camels* replaces "damsels." As a result, in Genesis 24:61, "Rebecca arose, and her camels, and they rode upon the camels."
- **The Affinity Bible:** In a list of family affinities, this 1927 edition tells us that "a man may not marry his Grandmother's wife." Glad that's cleared up.

THE
OLD TESTAMENT

the beginning: Genesis

What was the order in which God created the elements of the earth?

There are two creation accounts in the Bible — in Genesis 1 and 2, and the order is different in each account.

In Chapter 1, God creates the earth, then the plants, and then the animals, rather as if he's getting the earth ready for Adam and Eve, who comes last. In Chapter 2, God creates Adam and then plants a garden watered by rivers for Adam's use. Then come the animals and birds, and Adam is given the task of naming them. It is only when Adam still lacks a companion that God creates woman out of Adam's rib.

Some Biblical scholars think that this is a result of two different accounts being later combined by a compiler. Others feel that the two accounts are simply included to underline the importance of the event by the use of a literary device: first comes the big picture, then the detail.

TEN LONGEST NAMES IN THE BIBLE

1. Mahershalalhashbaz, "making speed to the spoil; he hastens to the prey" (Isaiah 8:1–3)
2. Chushanrishathaim, "blackness of iniquities" (Judges 3:8–10)
3. Bashanhavothjair, "the towns of Jair" (Deuteronomy 3:14)
4. Chepharhaammonai, "town of Benjamin" (Joshua 18:24)
5. Kibrothhattaavah, "the graves of lust" (Numbers 11:34; Deuteronomy 9:22)
6. Selahammahlekoth, "rock of divisions" (I Samuel 23:28)
7. Abelbethmaachah, "mourning to the House of Maachah" (I Kings 15:20; II Kings 15:29)
8. Almondiblathaim, "hidden in a cluster of fig trees" (Numbers 33:46–47)
9. Apharsathchites, "dividing or rending" (Ezra 4:9)
10. Helkathhazzurim, "the field of strong men, or of rocks" (II Samuel 2:16)

And the runners up:
- RamathaimZophim, "the two watch-towers" (1Samuel 1:1)
- Zaphnathpaaneah, "one who discovers hidden things" (Genesis 41:45)

What does the name *Adam* mean?

Adam means "man" in Hebrew. Interestingly, however, the name is a bit of a play on words. In Chapter 2 of Genesis, man is created "out of the dust of the ground." In Hebrew the word for ground is *adamah*.

What does the name *Eve* mean?

Adam first names his companion "Woman," because she was taken out of Man. However, after God announces that her punishment for her role in the Fall is, among other things, to bear children and to suffer while doing so, Adam renames her. He calls her "Eve," because "she was the mother of all living."

How did God create a woman out of Adam's rib and do men have fewer ribs?

Men don't have fewer ribs, though this has been suggested at times by the very literal. In fact, the creation account uses a Hebrew word that means "side" rather than "rib." A more widespread interpretation is that the rib incident simply underlines that man and woman are two halves of a whole, flesh of one flesh. In the creation account in Chapter 1, man and woman exist together from the first.

Adam's Rib

The movie *Adam's Rib*, released in 1949 and directed by George Cukor, was a vehicle for Katharine Hepburn and Spencer Tracy (in private life a couple equally matched in strength of character). Husband-and-wife lawyers, they end up battling on opposite sides in the trial of a wronged wife accused of taking a poorly aimed shot at her philandering husband. The "battle of the sexes" in the courtroom eventually spills over into the private lives of the married lawyers and comes close to "expelling" them from their heretofore happy marriage. The snake in this case is a predatory neighbour with an eye on Hepburn's character. Spencer Tracy, by the way, plays *Adam* Bonner. Get it?

How does "Adam's rib" relate to relations between the sexes?

Some people have interpreted the fact that Eve was created from Adam's rib to indicate that God intends woman to be subservient to man. Therefore, "Adam's rib" has often been invoked in the battle of the sexes.

Why was the fruit that Adam and Eve ate an apple?

The fruit that Adam and Eve ate is never identified. It is simply the fruit of the Tree of the Knowledge of Good and Evil and was forbidden to them by God's order. However, traditionally the fruit has been identified as an apple, and it's portrayed as an apple in songs, stories, and paintings. This idea was perhaps propagated by the fact that the Latin for *evil* and *apple* is the same word, differentiated only by accent.

Where did the term *Adam's apple* come from?

It was said that the forbidden fruit stuck in Adam's throat. Since the identification of the forbidden fruit with an apple has been so established, that lump in the male throat became known as an *Adam's apple*.

Why did God plant the tree in the Garden of Eden if he didn't want Adam and Eve to eat the fruit?

Theologians have suggested that this is much more than a tease. By giving Adam and Eve the choice to obey or disobey, God has emphasized a principle that is central to their humanity and, many would suggest, to their relationship with God: free will.

Where do we get the term *forbidden fruit*?

This now can be applied to anything that is not allowed. Although these exact words do not appear in the Bible, *forbidden fruit* refers, of course, to the fruit that God forbade Adam and Eve to eat in the Garden of Eden (Genesis 2). We all know how that turned out.

What other trees were in the Garden of Eden?

Well, only three are named. With the Tree of the Knowledge of Good and Evil, in the very centre of the garden, was the Tree of Life, which promised everlasting life. In addition, we know that there was a fig tree, because Adam and Eve whip up "aprons" of fig leaves when they hear God approaching and realize they are naked. Before expelling them from the Garden of Eden, God replaces the fig leaves with coats of animal skins.

Why do snakes slither, according to the Bible?

For his part in tempting Eve, the serpent is sentenced by God to move on his belly forever ("upon thy belly shalt thou go, and dust shalt thou eat all the days of thy life"). God also ordains that there will be "enmity" between the woman, her offspring, and the snake. Over the years some have suggested that this explains why so many people fear snakes, but theologians think there is more going on. Many of them believe the serpent represents Satan and the evil that must be struggled against.

What is the first incident of sibling rivalry in the Bible?

After Adam and Eve are expelled from the Garden of Eden, they have two sons: Cain and Abel. Cain works the land and Abel is a shepherd. Cain brings some of his crops to offer to God, but Abel brings the firstborn of his flock, and the fatty portions at that. When God favours Abel's offering, Cain becomes jealous and later, when they are alone in the fields, he strikes his brother and kills him.

Two things are interesting here. First, it's strongly implied that God favours Abel's *attitude* over Cain's. Also, though it is often left out of the story, God takes Cain to task for his jealousy and points out that, if he does a better job, his offering will also be accepted. In spite of this, Cain proceeds with Plan A, proving that, like his parents, he hasn't learned to handle free will.

What is the Mark of Cain?

Am I My Brother's Keeper?

It's obvious what the expression "am I my brother's keeper" now means: am I responsible for others? It should also be obvious that the desired answer is yes. The use of the question in Genesis 4:9 is more sinister. Cain has just murdered his brother, Abel. When God asks where Abel is (knowing full well), this is Cain's "Who, me?" response.

The Mark of Cain

The Mark of Cain is a well-reviewed British TV film that was first broadcast in 2007, three years after the revelations of torture at Abu Ghraib prison. It tells the story of soldiers on duty in Iraq who take part in the beating and sexual humiliation of Iraqi prisoners. When their deeds follow them home to England and a scandal erupts, one of the young men commits suicide, while the lives of the others are marked forever.

After he has murdered his brother, Cain is cursed by God, who also tells him that he is now doomed to be a fugitive and a vagabond. Ever the whiner, Cain argues that the punishment is too much for him, since he will have no protection and will be set upon and killed by anyone he encounters. God places a mark (undefined) on Cain, so that those he encounters will know not to kill him for fear of drawing God's curse on themselves.

It is interesting that what was intended as a mark of protection has come to be used through the years as a sign of sin or evil, perhaps through confusion with the curse put on Cain by God.

Unfortunately, some traditions have used this confusion to identify the mark as black skin, although the mark is never described in the Bible. This, of course, has proved useful through the years in defending slavery and prejudice.

Who founded the first city?

Quickies
Did you know ...
- that *East of Eden* was used by John Steinbeck as the title for his novel in which one of the central themes is the betrayal of a brother?

After Cain is banished for the murder of Abel, he goes into "the land of Nod, on the East of Eden," and there he marries and has a son named Enoch. He also builds a city, which he names after his son.

How is the Land of Nod associated with children's nursery rhymes?

The use of the word *nod* for the bobbing or dipping of the head is Old English. In the eighteenth century, Jonathan Swift put the nodding of the head together with sleep for the first time and used "nod off" in *Gulliver's Travels* to mean to go to sleep. However, the pun on the Bible's Land of Nod was probably most memorably associated with children's bedtimes when Robert Louis Stevenson wrote his poem "The Land of Nod," in *A Child's Garden of Verses* (1885).

How many children did Adam and Eve have?

Although he certainly doesn't share billing with his brothers, Cain and Abel, another son, Seth, was born when Adam was 130 years old. Adam then lived another 800 years, begetting sons and daughters all the while. That's a lot of begetting.

Who is the oldest man recorded in the Bible?

Some of the ages given in the Bible, especially the early part, are staggering. The oldest man in the Bible is Methusaleh, a descendant of Seth, who is recorded as living 969 years. That's why we say "as old as Methusaleh" to describe someone or something that's very old.

What kind of boat is an ark?

Ark is an old-fashioned English word for a chest and was used to translate the Hebrew word *aron*. What that means, and what God wanted Noah to build, is a large box.

How large was the Ark in the Bible?

God is very particular about the size of the Ark. Noah is told to build an Ark of gopher wood and to line it with pitch or tar. It is to be 300 cubits long, 50 cubits wide, and 30 cubits high, with three storeys, large rooms, a door in its side, and a nice window.

How long is a cubit? This is an ancient measurement that's no longer used. It was arrived at by measuring from the tip of the elbow to the tip of the fingers (rather the way a yard was measured by the distance from the nose to the end of the outstretched arm). Those who have tried this say that a man of average size measures 18 inches from elbow to fingertip, which would make the Ark approximately 450 feet long, 75 feet wide, and 45 feet high. Still pretty cozy.

How many of each living thing did Noah take with him on the Ark?

According to persistent tradition and toys, pictures, songs, and nursery wallpaper, Noah took two of every living thing, male and female, onto the Ark, as is written in Genesis 6. However, if you keep reading, God gets more specific in Chapter 7. "Unclean" beasts are to be taken in twos, but "clean" creatures and "birds of the air" are to be taken by sevens (this seems to suggest that one of those clean beasts is going to be very lonely, but it actually means seven pairs).

Also in attendance, of course, were Mrs. Noah (no name was ever given), his three sons Shem, Ham, and Japheth, and their wives.

How long were Noah and his family on the Ark?

Forty days and forty nights were how long the rain fell. After that, Noah had to wait for the land to dry, which took about another year. Family togetherness must have been wearing thin.

Where did the Ark "land"?

According to the Bible, the Ark came to rest "upon the mountains of Ararat." In the Armenian and Western Christian traditions, the Ark landed on the highest peak in the Ararat range, Mount Masis (which is accordingly now known as Mount Ararat), located on the border of Turkey and Armenia. Eastern tradition identifies the mountain as Mount Judi in northwestern Iran.

Why is the dove with an olive branch in its beak a symbol of peace?

Noah, anxious to go ashore, had to make sure that the land was dry. First he sent out a raven. At the same time, it seems, he sent out a dove. The first time he sent it out, the dove was unable to find anywhere to land, and returned to the Ark. After seven days, Noah sent it out again, and this time the dove came back with an olive leaf. This showed Noah that the water was going down. After seven more days, he sent the dove out a third time, and she didn't return. This proved to Noah that the earth was dry, and they could disembark.

Once the family stepped onto dry land, Noah built an altar and offered thanks to God for their deliverance, making sacrifices from among all the "clean" beasts (now you know why he took extras). Pleased by this, God made a covenant with Noah never again to destroy mankind, and he set a rainbow in the sky to mark the fact that he had made peace with man.

So why has the dove become the symbol of peace and not the rainbow? Good question. Maybe it's easier to draw.

Why does the word *babble* refer to "confused or incoherent" speech?

After the flood, God commands Noah and his sons to "be fruitful and replenish the earth" (Genesis 9:1). By this, he means for them to spread out, but the boys and their descendants cluster together and build a city with a great tower. In an effort to make them disperse, God confuses their speech, so that they can no longer understand one another, and this ends the building projects. Finally the people scatter through the world, as God had planned.

The city became known as Babel "because the Lord did there confound the language of all the earth" (Genesis 11:9), and *balal* is the Hebrew word for "confuses." The tower in the city is known as the Tower of Babel.

> **Quickies**
> *Did you know ...*
> • that the word used for Babel is the same word that is used later in the Bible for Babylonia, a country that caused the Israelites much confusion by warring with them and finally taking them into captivity.

What is *tithing*, and where did it come from?

This standard of giving, in which people are expected to give to God one-tenth of their earnings, is referred to in several passages in the Bible, but the first mention is in Genesis.

Abraham ("father of many"), the patriarch to whom God promised the Promised Land, is approached by a priest-king named Melchizedek who never appears again. Wordlessly, Melchizedek presents bread and wine and gives Abraham a blessing. Abraham responds by giving the priest one-tenth of the spoils he has just taken in battle.

Where did the practice of circumcision come from?

God has made a covenant with Abraham, promising that he will found a great nation and be blessed with land, riches, and descendants. As one of the tokens of this covenant, God commands that every "man child" in Abraham's household be circumcised (we won't go into details) at the age of eight days. One might think that Abraham, who is pushing one hundred at the time, might plead an exemption, but he doesn't. He and all the males of his household comply, and the rest is history.

It isn't clear why circumcision was part of Abraham's covenant with God. Both hygiene and an aid to fertility have been suggested.

Why are the cities of Sodom and Gomorrah a symbol of sin and loose living?

One day, three mysterious visitors appear on Abraham's tent-step. They have some good news and some bad news. The good news is that Sarah, Abraham's wife, is finally to bear a son. The bad news is that they have come down (yes, they're angels) to investigate reports of the wickedness of Sodom and Gomorrah, two nearby cities that are notorious for the shenanigans of their inhabitants.

This is bad news for Abraham, since his nephew, Lot, now lives in Sodom and Gomorrah with his family. A good uncle, Abraham pleads with God to spare the cities, finally extracting a promise that God will spare them if He can find ten righteous souls living there.

It seems, however, that this was asking too much of the people of Sodom and Gomorrah, for, after angels warn Lot and his family to flee, God sends "fire and brimstone" to destroy the cities.

The names *Sodom* and *Gomorrah* are now shorthand for wickedness, and the phrase *fire and brimstone* has entered our language.

> **Lot's Wife**
>
> Although Lot and his family were warned not to look back as they fled Sodom and Gomorrah, Lot's wife could not resist and was turned instantly to a pillar of salt, which is still pointed out by enthusiastic and imaginative tour guides.
>
> In fact, it is thought the cities lay near the Dead Sea, which has a very high salt content. Salt deposits form a number of "pillars" in this region. Just pick one.

Why do we say someone has "sold their birthright for a mess of pottage"?

Well, we don't say it much any more, though it's more common in England. This expression means that someone has foolishly exchanged something valuable for something much less valuable, and it comes from the story of Isaac, Abraham's son.

Isaac and his wife, Rebekah, have twin sons, Esau and Jacob. Because Esau emerged first, he was technically the elder son, and in line to inherit the largest share of the family estate.

As they grow up, the two brothers show different interests. Esau spends time out hunting, while Jacob stays close to home. One day, Esau comes in from hunting very hungry and finds Jacob cooking red lentil stew, or pottage. An impetuous fellow, Esau decides he's fading fast and must have some of the stew right away, so the wily Jacob says he will sell it to Esau for his birthright. "What good is my birthright if I starve to death?" says Esau and chows down, thus losing something of great value.

Why is the flexible ladder on a ship, which allows people to climb up to the deck from a small boat, called a *Jacob's ladder*?

Jacob does not only acquire Esau's birthright, but he also cheats him of their father's blessing, which was one of the most precious things a father could bestow in the ancient world. He did all this with the help of their mother, showing a pretty impressive example of early parental favouritism.

Needless to say, when Esau finds out he swears vengeance, and, to get Jacob out of town, Rebekah suggests he go from Beersheba to her brother's place in their ancestral homeland to find a wife. While sleeping out en route, Jacob has a dream in which a stairway (in some translations a ladder) appears, stretching from heaven to earth. Angels climb up and down on the ladder and God stands at the top, blessing Jacob and promising him the land on which he has been sleeping. This causes a major change of heart in Jacob.

The term *Jacob's ladder* has entered popular culture, perhaps most notably in the spiritual "We Are Climbing Jacob's Ladder," where it represents a longing for Heaven, and in the titles of songs by rock groups (Rush is one example). It was also the title of a 1990 movie thriller.

And of course, for obvious reasons, it has given a name to that ladder up the side of a ship.

What colour was Joseph's coat — really?

Jacob repeated his mother's parenting mistake. Among his twelve sons, he favours Joseph, his first son by his favourite wife, Rachel (things got complicated in those large families). As a mark of this favour, he gives Joseph a fine coat. What colour was it? No one knows for sure, since no one knows the meaning of the Hebrew word that described it. Most often, it has been said to be "multicoloured," or "a coat of many colours." Andrew Lloyd Webber was making a reasonable guess when he called it "Technicolor" in *Joseph and His Amazing Technicolor Dreamcoat*.

Where did we get the expression "Living off the fat of the land"?

This originally meant living off the best and most abundant crops, but it has come detached from agriculture and now means living well and taking advantage of the best there is.

The earliest promise of high living came from the pharaoh of Egypt to Joseph (he of the many-coloured coat). In Genesis 45:18, Pharaoh tells Joseph to bring his family from Canaan to Egypt "and I will give you the good of the land of Egypt, and ye shall eat the fat of the land."

the books of Moses:
Exodus,
Leviticus,
Numbers,
Deuteronomy

Why did the Egyptian king (Pharaoh) order all newborn male babies born to the Israelites to be thrown into the Nile River?

When Joseph's father and brothers first came to Egypt they were protected by Joseph's high-ranking position. However, years passed and Joseph and his generation were forgotten. The descendants of Joseph and his brothers have multiplied, and now are threatening to become what we might call a "critical mass."

The new Pharaoh is worried that they will one day rise up and take over the country or will join with one of Egypt's enemies to fight against their adopted country. First he tries oppressing them by making them slaves to work on his projects, but they continue to multiply.

Pharaoh takes sterner measures (Exodus 1). He orders the midwives to kill every newborn Hebrew male that they deliver. Cleverly, the midwives claim that Hebrew women are so quick to give birth that the babies have been delivered before the midwives arrive.

Growing even more frustrated, Pharaoh instructs his people to throw any male Hebrew babies into the Nile.

What does the name *Moses* mean?

Moses is a name that means something in both Hebrew and Egyptian.

To save Moses from death, his mother puts him in a reed basket lined with pitch to keep it afloat and places him in the bulrushes by the river's edge. There he is found by Pharaoh's daughter, who is moved by his cries and spares his life. Later she adopts him, giving him the name Moses, from the Hebrew word for "to draw out," since she drew him out of the water.

It is interesting that Pharaoh's daughter gives Moses a name of Hebrew origin, since *Moses* was also a common Egyptian name, meaning "son of." Given Moses' youth growing up in Pharaoh's court, this worked out well.

Who wrote the song
"Oh! Let My People Go"?

This is a traditional spiritual inspired by Moses' request to Pharaoh in Genesis 5: "Thus saith the Lord God of Israel, Let my people go." However, the first recorded use of the song was as a rallying song for the Contrabands, a large encampment of escaped slaves who gathered in Fort Monroe, Virginia, early in the Civil War. It had been the law that escaped slaves were to be returned to their owners, but the commander of the fort, General Butler, refused to return them, arguing that since Virginia had just declared itself a foreign power from the United States, the escaped slaves were contraband of war.

Sheet music followed, entitled The Song of the Contrabands: "O Let My People Go," though it was stated at the time that this was an arrangement of an 1853 song.

"Go Down Moses," a traditional spiritual, contains "Let my people go" as a refrain, so it's easy to assume that the roots of both songs are connected (the titles are used interchangeably on occasion). The opening verse of this song was published by the Jubilee Singers in 1872. William Faulkner's book of linked stories about a Southern family was entitled *Go Down Moses*, after the song.

The connection of the phrase with a release from slavery is obvious.

Which Pharaoh is it that
"lets the people go"?

Like so much else, this is a matter that scholars debate. One theory holds that the exodus takes place during the reigns of Seti I or his son, Rameses II, since at this time major building was taking place. Not only does the Bible describe this sort of activity, but slaves would have been necessary for the projects.

Where did the expression "Bricks with no straw" come from?

To make bricks with no straw means to be expected to accomplish something without being given the proper means to do so.

When Moses returned to Egypt, after living in Midian, God commanded that he ask Pharaoh to let his people, the Jews, go (thus giving rise to another well-known saying). Pharaoh, who counted on the labour of the Jews, did not react well to this. Instead, he ordered that conditions be made even more difficult for the Jews. For one thing, they were not to be supplied with the straw needed to make the bricks they used for building; they would have to cut their own straw. To make bricks without straw has therefore come to describe a task that has been made even more difficult because the necessary materials have been withheld.

To quote Pharaoh in Genesis 5:7 and 9: "Ye shall no more give the people straw to make brick, as heretofore: let them go and gather straw for themselves" and "let there more work be laid upon the men, that they may labour therein...." Sound familiar, *Dilbert* fans?

What failing does Moses claim in order to get out of the task of confronting Pharaoh?

Moses claims that he doesn't have the "gift of the gab." In Exodus 4:10, he says, "I am not eloquent ... I am slow of speech, and of a slow tongue." This might be rather endearing to some, but it simply irritates God. "Who do you think made your mouth?" He says, in effect. (It has been suggested that Moses was, in fact, a stutterer.)

God then suggests that Moses take his brother along: "Is not Aaron the Levite thy brother? I know that he can speak well." Thus Moses and Aaron become a brother act.

> **Quickies**
> *Did you know ...*
> • that in his famous movie *The Ten Commandments* (1956), Cecil B. DeMille considered having Charleton Heston's Moses stammer, but Heston couldn't pull it off. They settled on having him speak slowly.

What are the plagues that God inflicts on Egypt?

In order to force Pharaoh to release the Israelites from slavery, God visits ten plagues on Egypt (Exodus 7:12):

1. The Nile is turned to blood.

2. Frogs come out of the Nile and cover the land.

3. Egypt is swarmed by lice.

4. Egypt is swarmed by flies.

5. The livestock is killed by an unspecified disease (but not the livestock of the Israelites).

6. The Egyptians and their animals break out in boils.

7. Hail destroys most of the Egyptians' crops and their livestock.

8. Locusts descend on any of the crops that escaped the hail.

9. A darkness "that can be felt" covers Egypt for three days, though the homes of the Jews have light.

10. The firstborn of all the Egyptian families is slain, even Pharaoh's firstborn, by an angel of death. Each firstborn calf is killed as well.

What is the origin of Passover?

On the night before the firstborn are to be slain, Moses tells the Israelites to kill a lamb, take the blood, and place it on the two sideposts and the lintels of each home, and then to stay indoors until morning. The blood marks the homes of the Israelites, so, when God's destroying angel comes to strike the firstborn, the homes of the Israelites are *passed over*.

God commands that this sacrifice be re-enacted in perpetuity, in commemoration of his act of deliverance.

How long were the Israelites in Egypt?

According to the Bible, the Israelites spent 430 years in Egypt. The Bible also says in Exodus 12:41 that they left on the anniversary of the day they went into Egypt: "And it came to pass at the end of the four hundred and thirty years, even the selfsame day it came to pass, that all the hosts of the Lord went out from the land of Egypt."

How many Israelites left Egypt?

According to Exodus 12:37, the Israelites numbered about 600,000 on foot, plus children and "a mixed multitude." All told, the group that Moses led out of Egypt seems to have been pushing one million.

What is the body of water the Israelites cross to finally escape from Pharaoh's pursuit?

After the Israelites leave, Pharaoh has second thoughts. Perhaps his memory of plagues and death is short. Also, his own people are complaining, since the Israelites, who did most of the heavy work, are gone. "Why have we done this, that we have let Israel go from serving us?" they ask. These people are very slow learners.

And so Pharaoh set out after the Israelites with six hundred chariots and his army and comes upon them camped by a body of water. The Israelites are terrified, but Moses, commanded by God, holds his rod out over the water and God holds the Egyptians back with his pillar of fire and sends a strong wind that parts the water. The Israelites pass through, but when the Egyptians try to follow, God again tells Moses to stretch out his rod, and the waters cover the Egyptians, drowning them all.

There has been considerable debate about what body of water is involved in this story. Tradition says it was the Red Sea, since that was the way the name was translated in Greek. However, the Hebrew Bible calls the water in question "the sea of reeds."

What is manna?

As the Israelites wandered in the desert, they complained constantly, and one of the things they complained about was the lack of food. When Moses raised the issue with God, God promised that He would send flesh in the evening and "bread" in the morning.

Sure enough, according to Genesis 16:14, the next morning the ground was covered with "a small, round thing," for want of a better description.

TOP 10 MOST MENTIONED ANIMALS

1. Sheep: 188 times
2. Lamb or lambs: also 188
3. Horse or horses: 154
4. Ram or rams: 175
5. Ox or oxen: 166
6. Cattle: 153
7. Goat or goats: 132
8. Lion, lions, or lioness: 146
9. Ass or asses: 154
10. Bull, bulls, or bullock: 119

If we combine those that are similar, such as sheep and lambs, the next in line are:

Types of snakes — Serpent, serpents, viper, vipers, asp, asps: 66
Camel or camels: 62
Eagle or eagles: 34

As an interesting aside, the Bible also mentions these little-considered "biblical" animals: ferrets, chameleons, moles, cormorants, owls, and ravens.

Mystified, the Israelites asked, "What is it?" which in Hebrew is *"Manna?"*

Since they were to eat it for the next forty years, one hopes it was tasty. Exodus 16:31 says that "it was like coriander seed, white; and the taste of it was like wafers made with honey." Not bad.

> **Quickies**
> *Did you know ...*
> • that though manna seems to get top billing, God also promised "flesh" at night. This took the form of quails, which covered the Israelite camp.

Where did the word *fleshpots* come from?

The Israelites have been in the desert for a while, and they're hungry. They start complaining that they were better off in Egypt. As they say, "Would to God we had died by the hand of the Lord in the land of Egypt, when we sat by the flesh pots, and when we did eat bread to the full" (Exodus 16:3).

The flesh pots in Egypt were large cauldrons in which meat was boiled, and it is understandable that the Israelites, when longing for food, would think of these.

More recently, the word has come to mean (when it is used at all) the temptations of the flesh, particularly human flesh, as in "I hear you spent a weekend enjoying the fleshpots of Toronto."

Why did Moses break the first two stone tablets containing the Ten Commandments?

While Moses is spending forty days and forty nights receiving the laws from God on Mount Sinai, or, according to some, on Mount Horeb, his brother Aaron is back in camp, dealing with the unruly Israelites. Starting to believe that Moses has let them down and is not coming back, they plead with Aaron to make them "gods" to lead them — thus showing that Pharaoh wasn't the only slow learner.

Without further ado, Aaron collects all the gold earrings in the camp and fashions a golden "calf" (actually a bull; ancient peoples

Quickies

Did you know ...

- that the Ten Commandments are not the only laws Moses received from God on Mount Sinai? In fact, God laid out a heavy-duty roster of 613 laws.

didn't fool around with calves), to which the people bring offerings. One thing leads to another, and soon a rip-roaring party is going on.

Of course, this is when Moses returns from the mountain, clutching the two tablets on which are the Ten Commandments, "written with the finger of God" (Exodus 31:18). Moses, in a fit of anger, throws down the tablets of stone and smashes them. Luckily, after Moses has calmed down, God makes him two more tablets.

But Moses doesn't stop there. He then burns the golden calf, grinds it to powder, sprinkles it on water, and makes the people drink the mixture.

What is the order of the Ten Commandments?

For a confirmation of this handy checklist, see Exodus 20.

1. Thou shalt have no other gods before me.

2. Thou shalt not make unto thee any graven image (meanwhile the Israelites are breaking #2 back in camp).

3. Thou shalt not take the name of the Lord in vain (something to remember next time you drop something on your foot).

4. Remember the Sabbath day, to keep it holy.

5. Honour thy father and thy mother (even if they ground you).

6. Thou shalt not kill.

7. Thou shalt not commit adultery.

8. Thou shalt not steal.

9. Thou shalt not bear false witness against thy neighbour (i.e., lie).

10. Thou shalt not covet (anything belonging to anyone else).

Why does Michelangelo's famous statue of Moses have horns?

This is especially confusing to modern viewers, who connect horns with the devil and something bad. However, this is a result of a hiccup in translation.

When Moses comes down from Mount Sinai carrying the two stone tablets, the King James Version reads: "and when he came down from the mount, that Moses wist not that the skin of his face shone while he talked with him. And when Aaron and all the children of Israel saw Moses, behold, the skin of his face shone; and they were afraid to come nigh him" (Exodus 34:29–30). The Hebrew word that the KJV translated as "shone" is *qaran*, which usually meant "horns," but could also mean "radiant." The Latin Vulgate Bible was the Bible with which Michelangelo would have been familiar when he was sculpting Moses in 1515. Hence the horns.

> **The Wicked Bible**
>
> In 1631, thanks to a careless typesetter and a missing "not," people in England were briefly commanded to commit adultery. As soon as the error was discovered, Charles I ordered the printing destroyed (spoilsport). This edition has since been dubbed, "The Wicked Bible."

> **Quickies**
> *Did you know ...*
> • that the famous 1956 movie *The Ten Commandments*, starring Charlton Heston as Moses, was the second movie by that name directed by Cecil B. DeMille. The first was filmed in 1923.

What was the Ark of the Covenant?

The Israelites repent of their mistake with the golden calf/bull, and God restates his pledge to protect them. He then orders that they make a tabernacle, or sort of tent, that would become the centre of their worship of Him, and a sort of "residence" for God on the journey. Only priests could enter the tabernacle, and even they could enter the back section of the tent (called the Holy of Holies) only once a year. In the Holy of Holies rested the Ark of the Covenant.

This was a box of wood (acacia wood, if anyone was wondering) covered with gold, with a gold lid and two *cherubim* to guard it, one at each end facing each other. Inside were the Ten Commandments.

How did the book of Leviticus get its name?

This book is concerned mainly with the laws and special rituals that marked out the people of Israel as God's Chosen People, and it was the priestly tribe of Israel, the *Levites*, that put them into effect.

What is a scapegoat?

Leviticus 16:7–10 describes how, on the Day of Atonement, Aaron the High Priest is to take two goats and cast lots on them, one for God and one for the scapegoat. The goat on which God's lot falls is to be sacrificed as a sin offering, while the scapegoat is presented to God alive to make atonement and then sent into the wilderness carrying the sins of the people. No good news for the goats.

Today the term has come to mean one person in a family or a group who is singled out for undeserved blame or punishment, often to absolve the others from any sense of guilt.

Indiana Jones and the Ark of the Covenant

In the 1981 Steven Speilberg film, *Raiders of the Lost Ark*, professor and archaeologist Indiana Jones is contacted by U.S. Army intelligence officers. It is 1936, and the Nazis, in an effort to enlist its occult power in their rise to supremacy, are searching for the lost Ark of the Covenant. The agents enlist Indiana Jones to find the Ark and recover it before the Nazis, promising that it will be finally displayed properly in a museum.

As those who have seen the film know, Indiana finds the Ark in Tanis, Egypt, but the Nazis eventually end up with it in their possession. There they make a mistake. While our hero and his companion cover their eyes, the Nazis open the Ark and are destroyed by its power. When Indiana Jones carries the Ark back to the United States, government officials tell him that it has been taken "somewhere safe" for study. In reality, it has been stored in a government warehouse in an anonymous crate, and in effect lost again.

The Ark in the movie resembles very closely to the Ark described in the Bible, and the Israelites believed that carrying the Ark into battle made them invincible, since it was a sign that God was with them. This ties in with the efforts of the Nazis to acquire the Ark as the world drew closer to war.

The movie also draws on Biblical and archaeological scholarship when it has Indiana Jones discover the Ark in Tanis in Egypt.

Scholars speculate about the location of the Ark of the Covenant, but in fact no one is sure. Because a later pharaoh, Shishak I, is said to have attacked Judah and "taken away everything," one theory is that he took the Ark to his capital in Egypt: Tanis. This is the theory that Spielberg chose.

The Talmud suggests that the Ark was hidden under the Temple in Jerusalem, and is presumably still there, while an account in the Apocrypha has Jeremiah the prophet hiding it on Mount Nebo. Meanwhile Ethiopian Christians, drawing on an Ethiopian source, believe that King Solomon and the Queen of Sheba had a son, Menelik, who carried the Ark to Ethiopia. This tradition has it resting under the Church of Mary Zion in Aksum.

What is kosher?

As mentioned earlier, Noah was to take extra animals into the Ark if they were "proper." This is the meaning of the word *kosher*, and it also means that they are fit to be eaten. The dietary laws in the Bible are very specific about the animals, birds, fish, and "creeping things" that meet with approval. It is also only "clean," or proper, animals that can be offered as a sacrifice to God.

What is considered kosher?

No animals that have died of natural causes or are less than eight days old can be eaten. Animals that are *ruminants* and *ungulates* (translation: has an extra stomach and chews its cud, and has a split, or "cloven," hoof) are fair game. There are a few animals that try to pass for kosher, but aren't, such as rabbits, camels, and pigs. Only water critters that have fins and scales are kosher, and birds that don't eat flesh. Reptiles are out — though few are sorry about that. Some insects made the grade, but only if they have wings and leg joints that allow them to hop.

In addition, those who keep kosher do not eat meat and milk products together. One aspiring but insensitive politician won a place on the news when, on a tour of New York's garment district, he stopped for a corned beef sandwich and a glass of milk.

This can be traced to a prohibition that appears three times in the Bible against boiling a baby goat in its mother's milk (although there have been several explanations for the reason behind this).

Why do we say, "An eye for an eye and tooth for a tooth"?

This phrase ends several of the laws given to Israel. On the face of it, this seems to mean that every wrong that is done should be met with a corresponding punishment, and it is often used to justify vengeance. Interestingly, however, the phrase was originally meant to *limit* retaliation. One was forbidden to do more in retaliation than the wrongdoer had done initially.

Later, in the New Testament (Matthew 5:38), Jesus quotes this teaching. However, those who (mis)use it often misunderstand that Jesus, far from recommending the practice, is saying that people should go further and not retaliate at all. Jesus is saying, "Don't do this. Instead, turn the other cheek."

Who had the longest bed in the Bible?

Deuteronomy 3:11 tells us that "only Og king of Bashan remained of the remnant of giants; behold his bed was a bedstead of iron … nine cubits was the length was the length thereof, and four cubits the breadth of it." Taking our calculations from the measurement of the Ark in the last chapter, we know a cubit is roughly 18 inches long. That makes Og's bed some thirteen and a half feet long.

Why do the logos of many medical organizations use a snake curled around a rod?

As they wander in the desert, the Israelites continue to complain about their fate (forty years *is* a long time, after all). As a punishment for their lack of faith, God sends fiery serpents to bite the people, causing many deaths.

Yet again, the Israelites repent, and they go to Moses to intervene with God on their behalf. God tells Moses to make a serpent and put it on a pole. Anyone who is bitten and looks at the serpent will be saved. Moses obediently fashions a serpent out of brass and sets it on a pole, "and any man, when he beheld the serpent of brass, he lived."

Many believe this is the origin of the association of the serpent on the rod with healing and therefore with medical organizations, such as the American Medical Association.

There is an alternate explanation, however. The symbol of Asclepius, the Greek god of healing, is a snake and staff. In fact, the snake and staff is known in the language of symbols as "the rod of Asclepius."

Complicating matters further, the *caduceus*, which is two snakes wrapped around a wand, is often used mistakenly as a symbol for doctors and medicine, although it has no association with healing and medicine. It is associated in Greek myths with Iris, the messenger of Hera, and with Hermes, the messenger of the gods (and with Mercury in Roman myth).

What does the name *Deuteronomy* mean?

The actual meaning is "second law," but "second" means "repeated" in this case. Before Moses dies, he addresses the people he has led so long, reminding them of God's deliverance and the laws that have been settled on as part of their covenant with God. This means that Deuteronomy serves as a sort of review of the previous forty years and a recap of important laws, such as the Ten Commandments.

Where is Moses buried and who buried him?

Moses is forbidden by God to enter the Promised Land of Canaan, but as a mark of favour, God allows him to see it before he dies. Moses climbs Mount Nebo in Moab, God shows him the land that he will give to the Israelites, and then Moses dies at the age of 120. As a sign of their bond, God himself buries Moses in Moab, but "no man knoweth of his sepulchre unto this day" (Deuteronomy 34:6).

getting settled: the books of Samuel, Kings, and Chronicles

What do the judges Samuel and Samson have in common?

Like Samson, Samuel is dedicated to God at his birth. In doing so, their mothers took what is known as a "Nazirite vow" on behalf of their children. As with Samson, Samuel is forbidden to cut his hair, eat meat, or drink alcohol.

It has to be said that Samuel does a much better job of keeping his vow than Samson the party boy.

What was King Saul's most noticeable physical characteristic?

The Bible makes very clear that Saul was unusually tall. In I Samuel 9:2, it is recorded that "from his shoulder and upward he was higher than any of the people." Shortly after, in I Samuel 10:23 Saul is brought before Samuel, and "he was higher than any of the people from his shoulders and upward." Even in the Bible, it seems, tall men are more successful.

What do we mean by "a man after one's own heart"?

We use this to refer to someone who shares one's views and values. It comes from I Samuel 13:14, where Samuel, the high priest, delivers a warning to King Saul. Saul has messed up big time, and God has sought out someone to take his place — someone who lives according to God's laws. He is a man after God's heart. This refers to David, who is soon anointed king.

What was David's special talent?

David, who would succeed Saul, was well-known for his musical ability. In fact, this is what earns him a place in the royal palace (according to one version of the story).

By this point Saul has angered God, and God has sent an evil spirit to torment him. His servants decide that "a man who is a cunning player on an harp" should be called in to play for Saul and soothe him in his worst moments. Word of David's talent has spread, so he is summoned to the royal household — with his harp. He and Saul hit it off right away, and David's playing has the desired effect, calming Saul. He is promoted to armour-bearer for Saul, and plays for him whenever the evil spirit takes possession of him. (Scholars have speculated that Saul was suffering some form of mental illness.)

The harp in question, by the way, was not the grand and bulky instrument we know today, but a lyre, a small, portable harp.

What do we mean by a "David and Goliath" contest?

This refers to a contest in which the two protagonists are far from evenly matched. There is also an implication that the smaller of the two is the favoured one, and the underdog will be victorious. Julia Roberts doing battle with polluting corporations in the movie *Erin Erin Brockovich* would be a prime example.

> **Quickies**
> *Did you know ...*
> • that it is traditionally believed that many of the Psalms were written by David. They are, after all, religious verses set to music.

> **Quickies**
> *Did you know ...*
> • that in the 1953 film *David and Bathsheba*, Goliath was played by a Polish wrestler named Wladyslaw Talun?

The expression comes from I Samuel 17, in which the Israelites are (again) fighting the Philistines. The Philistines have put forward a champion, Goliath, who is challenging the Israelites to send someone to battle with him one-on-one. If the Israelite champion wins, the Philistines will become servants of the Israelites, but if Goliath wins, the Israelites will serve the Philistines.

Now, Goliath is no ordinary contender. First of all, he is enormous. The Bible sets his height at "six cubits and a span." Depending on whether you accept the Hebrew or the Greek interpretation of this, he is either 9 feet 9 inches tall or a puny 6 feet 9 inches. On top of that, he is armoured and armed to the teeth, like something out of *Terminator*.

Goliath has been strutting around and trash-talking for forty days when David, who has been home visiting the family, arrives in the Israelite camp with supplies for his soldier brothers. Outraged at the insult to Israel, he asks Saul if he can take up Goliath's challenge.

Although Saul offers his royal armour, David declines and goes out to meet Goliath armed only with a staff, a sling, and five smooth stones.

Goliath, of course, can hardly believe his eyes, but David runs towards him, places a stone in his sling, and hurls a stone straight at Goliath's forehead. When Goliath falls to the earth, David cuts off his head with Goliath's own sword. Exit Goliath.

David takes Goliath's head back to Saul as a token of victory. Though this was a gruesome souvenir, it was probably not as cringe-making as the two hundred foreskins that he was to bring back from another battle.

When Michelangelo sculpted his famous figure of David for the city of Florence, Italy, it is this chapter in David's history that he chose to portray: David stands, looking determined, his sling thrown over his shoulder. Of course, Michelangelo has taken certain artistic licence, since in the sculpture David is naked (Donatello takes the same licence with his statue of David). Although he declined Saul's armour, there is no evidence that David went into his contest with Goliath *au naturel*.

Interestingly, the Florentines, fiercely independent, placed the statue so it glared in the direction of Rome.

How did Saul's children save David's life?

> **Quickies**
> *Did you know ...*
> • that, David and Goliath were also portrayed by Caravaggio and Gustave Doré?

As David's fame as a fighter grows, so does Saul's jealousy — and Saul is not one to keep his feelings to himself. In fact, once, as David plays the lyre in his presence, Saul throws a javelin at him. It misses, but David gets the message.

Luckily for David, Saul's children are on David's side. David had married Saul's daughter Michal. (In fact, he had brought back the two hundred foreskins to win her hand. So romantic.) When Saul sends "messengers" to

David's house to kill him, Michal lets David down to safety out a window and then places a bolster in his bed to deceive them, simultaneously influencing the plot of countless suspense thrillers in the process.

Jonathan, Saul's son, is David's best friend. At one point, David is (wisely) hiding out "in the field." Jonathan says he will feel out his father out on the subject of David and then let David know if it is safe to return. He plans a signal. When he determines his father's feelings, he will come out and fire three arrows. If he tells his servant that the arrows have fallen on the near side of David's hiding place, David (who is listening) will know it is safe. If, however, he tells the servant to fetch the arrows from beyond David's hiding place, David will know to get out of town.

Saul's mood, unfortunately, has not improved, so David flees. Jonathan's farewell — "The Lord be between thee and me for ever" — became a much-used expression.

Who is the Witch of Endor?

Samuel, the priest/judge who anointed Saul king, dies, and on the verge of another battle with the Philistines, Saul is feeling a bit insecure (and a little lonely, no doubt, given the way he's alienating people). He decides to seek out a medium to try to contact Samuel in the afterlife to ask how the battle will turn out.

Quickies
Did you know ...
- that "David and Jonathan" was once commonly used to describe a pair of devoted male friends. The expression seems to have fallen out of use.

On inquiring of his servants, he learns that there is a medium at Endor, so he puts on a disguise (not out of fear, but because he himself had outlawed all supernatural practices) and approaches the woman.

Samuel is not very happy to be hauled back. "Why hast thou disquieted me?" he asks (I Samuel 28:15). Nor does he have good news for Saul. Saul has lost God's favour, and in the battle the Philistines will triumph and Saul and his sons will be killed. Obviously they don't pull their punches in the afterlife.

The woman is actually never called the Witch of Endor in the Bible. She is referred to as "a woman that hath a familiar spirit." However, she seems to have caught the imagination of writers and artists throughout the centuries, and the Witch of Endor she will remain.

Where do we get the expression "How are the mighty fallen"?

This is used to mean that those who were once powerful are now overthrown or reduced in circumstances. Though it is sometimes tempting to quote this phrase when a notoriously offensive person falls on hard times, in the Bible it was part of a lament, and a particularly beautiful one at that.

In II Samuel 1, David is brought word that both King Saul and his son Jonathan are dead. Now, although Saul resented David and had tried to have him killed, he had once been good to David, and Jonathan and David were dear friends. What is more, Saul was God's anointed king. So David tears his clothes and mourns, saying (Verse 19), "The beauty of Israel is slain upon thy high places: how are the mighty fallen."

TOP 10 MOST COMMON NOUNS IN THE BIBLE

1. Lord: 7,365 occurrences
2. God: 4,293
3. Man: 2,747
4. Israel: 2,509
5. People: 2,271
6. King :2,124
7. Son: 1,980
8. Men: 1,860
9. House: 1,840
10. Day: 1,759

When did Jerusalem become the capital of Israel?

Establishing his capital in Jerusalem (c. 1000 B.C.E.) is one of David's first moves when he becomes king. David is uniting Judah and the northern tribes to form one kingdom, the Kingdom of Israel, and moving the capital from Hebron in Judah to a city that is close to

the border between the two territories is wise practice. He also trans-
fers the Ark of the Covenant, the centre of religious life, to Jerusalem.

Who was the original heir to David's throne?

If you thought it was Solomon, you're not alone — but you're wrong.

The heir to David's throne is originally the crown prince, Amnon.
However, Amnon makes the mistake of falling in love with his half-sister Tamar. He then makes the even bigger mistake (to put it mildly) of
arranging to have Tamar come to his room, and raping her. A slimeball
to his fingertips, he then turns on Tamar, saying, "Arise, be gone," and
ordering his servants, "Put now this woman out from me, and bolt the
door after her" (II Samuel 13:17). A real prince.

When he finds out about this, Absalom, Tamar's full brother, plots
revenge. He bides his time, waiting two years, then holds a big shindig.
When Amnon is "merry with wine" Absalom has his servants kill him.

Who is Zadok the Priest, and why did Handel write an anthem about him?

When David moves the capital to
Jerusalem and unites the Kingdom of
Israel, he also has to decide which of
two groups of priests should have pre-
cedence. One group is led by Abiathar,
and traces its roots back to Moses, and
the other group is led by Zadok, and
claims descent from Aaron, Moses'
brother. David wisely refuses to choose,
and appoints both Abiathar and Zadok
as High Priest.

Quickies
Did you know ...
• that one of the soldiers with which David did battle had twelve fingers and twelve toes? II Samuel 21:20 reads: "And there was yet a battle in Gath, where was a man of great stature, that had on every hand six fingers, and on every foot six toes, four and twenty in number."

Time passes. As David lies dying, two of his sons are jockeying
for position: Adonijah, now the eldest son, and Solomon, who has the

61

Absalom and Literature

Absalom has come to represent the rebellious son. After the death of the crown prince — and Absalom's half-brother — Amnon, Absalom sets out to depose his father, King David. When he feels he has enough public support, he declares himself king, forcing David to flee from Jerusalem. As if that isn't enough, in a calculated act of disdain, he proceeds to sleep with David's concubines. In public.

Finally, however, his troops are defeated by David's, and it is Absalom's turn to flee. Even then, David, the fond father, pleads with his soldiers to treat Absalom gently, and when Absalom is nevertheless killed by the captain of the army, Joab, David mourns with the famous words, "O my son Absalom, my son! my son! Would I had died instead of you, O Absalom, my son, my son!"

This theme of struggle and tortured affection between father and son seems to have spoken to a number of writers — interestingly, most of them men.

Perhaps the first was John Dryden, writing in 1681–82. He fashioned the story into an allegorical political satire in verse, *Absalom and Achitophel*, in which he deals with political events of the day, such as the Monmouth Rebellion. In his work, the Duke of Monmouth, Charles II's illegitimate son who had attempted to seize the throne, becomes Absalom, and the fond king and father, Charles II, is portrayed as David. There are quite a few other renditions:

- Rainer Maria Rilke makes reference to Absalom in two poems, "Absalom's Rebellion" and "Absalom's Abfall."
- William Faulkner explores the theme of a son, Henry Sutpen, rebelling against his father's values in *Absalom, Absalom!* (1936).
- Popular novelist Howard Spring deals with a father's devotion to a spoiled and selfish son in his 1940 novel *My Son, My Son!* which was made into a film by the same name, also in 1940. The novel's original title was *O Absalom*.
- In Alan Paton's 1948 novel *Cry, the Beloved Country*, Stephen Kumalo and his son Absalom struggle over many issues in pre-apartheid South Africa. Like the biblical Absalom, Absalom Kumalo dies an untimely death, executed for murder.
- In *The Manticore* (1972), the middle volume of his Deptford Trilogy, Robertson Davies uses the David-Absalom story throughout to comment on the fraught relationship between the protagonist and his father. He even introduces a new term, "Absalonism," to describe a son's rebellion against his father.

These are just some of the better known references to the Absalom story in literature. For a thorough rotter, Absalom seems to have made quite a mark.

backing of his mother, Bathsheba. As the favourite wife, Bathsheba still has influence with David, and she convinces him to name Solomon as his successor, throwing Adonijah and his followers into confusion.

Unfortunately for Abiathar, he has backed the wrong candidate and is stripped of his office, leaving Zadok as High Priest.

In I Kings 1:39, "Zadok the priest took an horn of oil out of the tabernacle, and anointed Solomon." Although he shared the task with Nathan the prophet, Zadok seems to have received top billing.

In 1727, George Frideric Handel used this text for one of four anthems he composed for the coronation of George II of England. It has been used in every coronation service since then, traditionally during the anointing of the new monarch.

Why is a wise person referred to as a "Solomon"?

When Solomon became king of Israel, God asked him what gift he would like. Solomon answered that he wished for "an understanding heart to judge thy people, that I may discern between good and bad" (I Kings 3:9). This pleases God, who grants his request.

Solomon's wisdom is soon put to the test in one of Bible's better known stories.

Two women come to him. They are "harlots" (they didn't mention that in Sunday school, did they?) who live in the same house and both had infants sons. One of them claims that the other woman rolled on her own son in the night, killing him. Then she took the first woman's boy secretly from her while she slept and claimed that it was hers. The second woman protests that this is a lie, and that the living child is her own. What to do?

Solomon calls for a sword. "We'll cut the boy in half," he says reasonably, "and then you can each have one part." One of the women is fine with this plan, but the other protests, saying that she will give up her claim if Solomon lets the child live.

"This is the mother," Solomon declares. As the Bible then says, "And all Israel heard of the judgement that the king had judged."

From then on, Solomon was known far and wide for his wisdom. I Kings 4:30–31 says that Solomon "was wiser than all men … and his fame was in all nations round about." He spoke 3,000 proverbs, had 1,005 songs in his repertoire, and could talk about animals, birds, trees, "creeping things," and fish. Too bad Trivial Pursuit wasn't invented.

Today, the *Oxford English Dictionary* lists an adjective, "Solomonic," taken from his name.

How many wives did Solomon have?

This is one place where Solomon's wisdom can be questioned. He had seven hundred wives and three hundred concubines, in case seven hundred wives weren't enough.

When did Solomon build the Temple in Jerusalem?

As usual with these things, there is some debate, but many scholars put the construction of the Temple around 960 B.C.E.

Was Solomon married to the Queen of Sheba?

There's nothing in the Bible to suggest a romance, let alone a marriage, though no one seems to have told this to Hollywood.

The tales of Solomon's wisdom and wealth travel as far as the kingdom of Sheba (thought to have been in modern-day Yemen or in Ethiopia), where the queen hears of him. In the biblical account, she is known only as the queen of Sheba, but she also appears in other traditions. The Ethiopians call her Makeda, and in the Islamic tradition of Arabia she is known as Balqis, in Roman history, Nicaule.

What seems evident is that she was a rich and powerful queen, who probably reigned in her own right (a queen regnant) and was not simply the consort of a king. She was also of an inquiring nature. When the accounts of Solomon reach her, she decides to find out for herself if they are true and sets out north in a sumptuous procession, carrying gold, jewels, and spices. When she arrives in Jerusalem, she doesn't waste any time but goes to Solomon and speaks to him "of all that was in her heart." In her heart, apparently, are ten questions, all of which Solomon answers frankly.

The Queen of Sheba in Film

It's no wonder that misconceptions surround the Queen of Sheba. In popular culture, she has been transformed from a powerful queen, willing to travel in search of wisdom, to a sultry temptress, ready to use men like Kleenex in pursuit of her desires.

The Queen of Sheba (1921), a silent film originally intended as a vehicle for famous vamp Theda Bara, stars Betty Blythe as a very scantily clad Queen, who looks more like a harem dancing girl than any sort of monarch. Blythe seems to have had a sense of humour about the whole thing, reportedly saying, "They made forty costumes for me, and if I had them all on at once, I would still be chilly in the desert."

Solomon and Sheba (1959) completely revised the story, having Sheba as an ally of the Egyptian Pharaoh in opposition to Solomon. She plots to seduce Solomon and introduce a pagan form of worship from her own country. The orgy scene shocked audiences of the day. The Queen, played by sultry Italian actress Gina Lollobrigida, is resolutely scantily clad, and the promotional material is plastered with Lollobrigida and co-star Yul Brynner (Solomon) in steamy poses. Tyrone Power was originally playing the role of Solomon, but dropped dead of a heart attack while filming a scene. He can apparently be seen in long shots in the movie.

In more recent years, the sultriness has been toned down, but the tale-spinning continues. *Solomon and Sheba*, a TV movie of 1995, stars Halle Berry as a plucky Queen Nikaule. Solomon has taken over her country's frankincense trade, and she sets off not to visit but to confront him. Berry's wardrobe is more modest (in fact, she dresses as a man at one point), but inevitably she and Solomon (Jimmy Smits) fall in love. By the way, Halle Berry was the first black woman to play the Queen of Sheba; Viveca A. Fox was next, in 1997, starring opposite Ben Cross as Solomon.

The queen is more than pleased. She confesses that she had not believed the accounts of Solomon's wisdom, but was now convinced. As she says, "the half was not told me: thy wisdom and prosperity exceedeth the fame which I heard" (I Kings 10:7). With these words, she makes a gift to Solomon of the gold, precious stones, and spices that she has brought with her. He, in turn, grants her anything she wishes "from his bounty." And she returns home.

Ethiopian tradition, on the other hand, does suggest a relationship between Solomon and the Queen, which produced a son, Menelik.

Why is a very large bottle of wine called a "Jeroboam"?

Quickies
Did you know ...
• that Handel composed his much-loved "Arrival of the Queen of Sheba" for his Oratorio *Solomon* in 1749.

In his later years, Solomon starts to alienate some of his people, specifically the northern tribes that his father, David, brought into a united kingdom with Judah. Finally they rebel, under their leader, Jeroboam. The rebellion is put down, and Jeroboam flees to Egypt (doesn't everyone?) until Solomon dies. However, he eventually becomes the first king of a separate Israel.

How does this relate to bottles of wine? No one is exactly sure, but biblical names have been applied to a number of the larger bottles. A magnum, as most know, is the rough equivalent of two bottles of wine, and the Jeroboam (also known as a double magnum) contains approximately four bottles. Other biblically named wine bottles are the Rehoboam (six bottles), the Methuselah (eight bottles), the Salmanazar (twelve bottles), the Balthazar (sixteen bottles), the Nebuchadnezzar (twenty bottles), the Melchior (twenty-four bottles), the Solomon (approximately twenty-eight bottles), and the Melchizedek (forty bottles). Today, the only term that can be used officially on a bottle of wine is the *magnum*.

The *Jeroboam* is one of the oldest of the terms, being used as early as 1725 in Bordeaux. One theory for the name is that Jeroboam is described as a "mighty man of valour" (I Kings 11:28), "who made Israel to sin" (I Kings 14:16).

Why is a wicked woman
referred to as a "Jezebel"?

After David dies, things go downhill, with turmoil, wars, assassination, and other bad behaviour.

The tenth King of Israel is a particularly nasty specimen named Ahab. What's more, he marries a Phoenician princess named Jezebel, who is as vile as her new husband. Not only do they encourage the worship of the Canaanite storm god, Baal, but they exploit their people terribly.

Of the two, Jezebel seems even more ruthless than her husband. On one occasion, Ahab is coveting a choice vineyard belonging to his neighbour, Naboth. "No problem," says Jezebel, and she bribes two men to testify that Naboth has cursed not only Ahab the king, but God. Naboth is executed and Ahab is happy.

However, while Ahab is inspecting his new property, God sends the prophet Elijah to confront him, predicting that "dogs will lick up your blood." This is exactly what happens to Ahab and Jezebel.

First, Ahab is killed in battle, dying in his chariot. As his chariot is being washed, dogs lick up his blood.

Jezebel's death is even more spectacular. During a bloody rebellion, Jezebel is trapped in the city of Jezreel by the new king, Jehu. As he rides into the city gate, Jehu sees Jezebel looking out a window. He orders some eunuchs who are with her to throw her out of the window, which they do. In a strikingly bloody scene, "some of her blood was sprinkled on the wall and on the horses: and he trod her under foot" (II Kings 9: 33). Even more gruesome is the scene when they return to bury "this cursed woman." All they find are her head, hands, and feet. She has been eaten by dogs.

One of the major strikes against Jezebel in the Christian tradition is her devotion to Baal, but there are also her idolatrous practices, and her evil influence in encouraging the king to turn away from God. However, in popular culture, she has become the symbol of an evil woman — particularly one that is dominating or sexually promiscuous ("a painted Jezebel"). This may be because she does her hair and puts on makeup when she sees Jehu (and her death) approaching. Some think this is an ill-fated attempt to seduce Jehu, but it was more likely a way of meeting death with dignity. She is a princess, after all.

In *Jezebel* (1938), Bette Davis tones down the promiscuity, playing a headstrong Southern belle whose hurtful choices ruin her chances at happiness. The Jezebel comparison is likely drawn from her controlling behaviour and from a ballroom scene in which she shows up in a scarlet dress to humiliate her fiancé, Henry Fonda. Young, unmarried women in the time didn't wear red unless they were of questionable morality, and the shameless dress brings the ball to a halt.

In his 1951 hit "Jezebel," Frankie Laine plays with the wicked image when he sings, "If ever the devil was born, / Without a pair of horns / It was you."

Who was the fastest sprinter in the Bible?

God's prophet, Elijah, challenges King Ahab's priests of Baal to a contest on Mount Carmel, where he defeats them roundly. He then slaughters them.

Not surprisingly, Ahab leaves to ride back to the city of Jezreel, but Elijah (who is no spring chicken) "girds up his loins" and beats the king to the city gate.

Why is a reckless driver known as a "Jehu"?

Jehu, formerly a military leader and then King of Israel, was known for his driving — but not in a good way. At one point, a watchman is standing on the walls of Jezreel, when he sees a "company" approaching. In answer to questions about who it is, he answers "the driving is like the driving of Jehu the son of Nimshi; for he driveth furiously" (II Kings 9:20).

Coachmen used to refer to a colleague who drove too fast or recklessly as a "Jehu."

Who was taken up to heaven in a fiery chariot?

This is another popular misconception. The prophet Elijah is travelling with Elisha, who is to be Elijah's successor, when they come to the Jordan River. In a scene reminiscent of the entry of the Israelites into the Promised Land, Elijah parts the river, so that they can cross over. Once they have done so, a fiery chariot drawn by horse of fire separates the two men, and

---

"Swing Low, Sweet Chariot"

"Swing low sweet chariot
Coming for to carry me home"

This well-known spiritual, which enjoyed new popularity during the folk revival and civil-rights struggle of the 1960s, has a complex history.

Although there is a belief that it was composed by an elderly black woman in Tennessee to comfort a fellow slave, the official story of its composition (c. 1862) attributes it to one Wallis Willis, a freedman who lived in the Choctaw Nation. He is said to have drawn inspiration from the Red River, which made him think of the Jordan River.

A minister at the Choctaw school, Alexander Reid, wrote down the words and music after hearing Willis singing this and an equally famous song, "Steal Away." Reid then sent both songs to the Jubilee Singers of Fisk University in Nashville, and they were the first group to record it in 1909. Did Willis compose it, or was he singing a traditional song that he remembered from his youth? History does not answer that question.

Opinion is divided on the meaning of the song as well. The spiritual interpretation would suggest that it is a longing to be taken home to Heaven by God, rather like the message in "Roll, Jordan, Roll." On the other hand, references to the Underground Railroad were often concealed in spirituals. It has been argued that "chariot" might refer to the Underground Railroad, "Jordan" to the Mason-Dixon Line, and "home" to freedom in the North. John Lovell Jr., author of *Black Song*, points out that Harriet Tubman, one of the leaders of the Railroad, was known by the nickname "Old Chariot."

The song has been sung by an impressive number of famous voices, including Benny Goodman (1936), Fats Waller (1938), Paul Robeson (1939), Peggy Lee (1946), Johnny Cash (1959), Harry Belafonte (1960), Stevie Wonder (1968), Joan Baez (1970), Eric Clapton (1975), Willie Nelson (1996), and Etta James (2000), and many others.

For decades, interestingly, the song has been used by English rugby fans.

Elijah is taken up to heaven in a whirlwind. Nonetheless, it is the chariot that lives on in songs and stories.

Who is the grouchiest bald man in the Bible?

One day, the prophet Elisha is going to Bethel. As he approaches it, "little children" (most likely youths with too much time on their hands) come out of the city and start to make fun of him, saying, "Go up, thou bald head." Does Elisha preserve a dignified silence? He does not. Instead he curses them, and two "she-bears" come out of the woods and tear forty-two of the children limb from limb.

Who had the longest reign of any king of Judah or Israel?

Manasseh, son of King Hezekiah, reigned for forty-five years, from 687 to 642 B.C.E.

When are the city of Jerusalem and the Temple destroyed and when does the Babylonian captivity begin?

The Babylonians under King Nebuchadnezzar have been warring with Israel and Judah for some time, and have been taking the elite of the land captive (at one time 10,000 were exiled). However, it is in 586 B.C.E. that the Babylonians finally conquer the city, raze the Temple built by Solomon, and carry off much of the population to Babylon. There they stay until King Cyrus gives them permission to return home in 539 B.C.E. By that point, almost two generations have passed, and only some take him up on his offer.

judges and priests: Joshua, Judges, and Ruth

Who was the prostitute who helped the Israelites conquer the Promised Land?

Moses' leadership is assumed by his right-hand man, Joshua, whose task it is to lead the Israelites into the Promised Land. One catch is that the land already has people living in it. In fact, right across the Jordan River from the Israelite camp is the Canaanite city of Jericho.

A canny leader, Joshua realizes that the inhabitants will not willingly surrender what they consider their property, so he sends two spies into Jericho to assess the situation. They, for reasons that remain speculative, take shelter in the house of a prostitute named Rahab.

Things do not go well. Someone tells the king of Jericho that there are Israelite spies in town. What is more, he seems to have fairly accurate information, because he sends a message to Rahab, ordering her to surrender the men.

Rahab thinks quickly. She hides the men on the roof of the house among some flax that she has set to dry. Then she says, in effect, "Sure, they were here, but they've gone. You'd better chase them."

As soon as the search party leaves the city in pursuit of the spies, Rahab, whose house is on the city wall, lets the two spies down to safety from a window.

Why does she do this? She — and everyone else — has heard of the Israelites' successes in battle, and she is convinced that God is with them and will deliver Jericho into their hands. She asks that she, her family, and all their possessions be spared when the Israelites take the city. The spies tell her to take the scarlet cord she used to let them down outside the walls and tie it in her window, and she and her family will be safe.

Why has crossing the Jordan River become associated with dying?

The Israelites are at this point not yet in the Promised Land, but they are camped on the shores of the Jordan River. All they have to do to enter the Promised Land is to cross the river.

In a scene that harks back to the Israelites' crossing of the Red/reed Sea, God tells Joshua to send priests ahead, carrying the Ark of the Covenant. As soon as their feet touch the water, the river parts to let the people walk across.

Particularly in countless spirituals, such as "Roll, Jordan, Roll" and "Cross Over to the Other Side of Jordan," this crossing has come to mean the passage from this life to the everlasting life of Heaven. To people for whom life was difficult, the prospect of the joys of Heaven must have appeared as much a deliverance as the passage of the Israelites from slavery in Egypt to the Promised Land of "milk and honey."

Underlining this meaning is a couplet that appears in many spirituals: "Jordan's River is chilly and cold / Chills the body but not the soul." This is called a *floating* or *zipper verse*, since it can float from song to song and be "zippered in."

Interestingly, later in the Bible, the prophet Elijah parts the River Jordan so he and his successor, Elisha, can cross over Jordan. Elijah is then taken up to Heaven.

Who did the Israelites finally bury in the Promised Land?

Several hundred years before, back in Genesis 50:24–26, Joseph predicts that God would eventually deliver the Israelites into the land that God promised to Abraham, and he asks the Israelites "to carry up my bones from hence." He is embalmed, and the Israelites are as good as their word, carrying him with them out of Egypt and into the desert, and finally burying him in their new land.

Joshua Fit de Battle of Jericho

The walls of Jericho were famous in the ancient world for their sturdiness, and Joshua must have wondered how his men would ever break through. However, God has instructions. The entire army is to circle the city once a day for six days. With the army should go seven priests with ram's-horn trumpets, leading the Ark of the Covenant. On the seventh day, they are to circle seven times, and then the priests are to make a loud blast on the trumpets, the people are to shout, and the walls will collapse. And that's what happens.

"Joshua Fit de Battle of Jericho" is an African-American spiritual that recounts the story of the fall of Jericho. Probably a product of the early nineteenth century, it reflects the slaves' dialect. Since the spirituals very often expressed a longing for freedom, the symbolism of the walls falling would have been significant.

This song was one of those popularized by singer Mahalia Jackson.

What is meant by *judges* in the Book of Judges?

TOP 10 LONGEST-LIVED PEOPLE IN THE BIBLE	
Name	Age
1. Methuselah	969
2. Jared	962
3. Noah	950
4. Adam	930
5. Seth	912
6. Kenan	910
7. Enos	905
8. Mahalalel	895
9. Lamech	777
10. Shem	600

The word in this context has nothing to do with Judge Judy and those like her. Judges in the ancient world were impressive leaders who ruled by force of personality and were also military commanders. Okay, so they might have heard a case now and again.

Judges weren't kings, however, because the title (in Hebrew, *shofet*) died with the individual judge, and a judge did not lead all the tribes of Israel at one time.

Who is the only left-handed person mentioned in the Bible?

In the course of the Book of Judges, the people of Israel continually turn to other deities, God punishes them by allowing them to be conquered by a foreign power, they repent, and God appoints a judge to save them. In the course of one of these periods of foreign oppression, the Israelites are labouring under the yoke of a Moabite king named Eglon, and their calls for deliverance cause God to send a judge named Ehud, who is left-handed, to liberate them.

At one point the Israelites must send a "present" (tribute) to Eglon. Ehud takes on the task of delivering the tribute, and fashions a cubit-long (eighteen inches), two-sided dagger, which "he did gird it under his raiment upon his right thigh" (Judges 3:16). The point here is that the guards who let Ehud into the presence of the king are going to check on Ehud's left side for a weapon, since that's where most (right-handed) men carry theirs.

Once they are alone, Ehud stabs the king and then locks the door to the room, allowing enough time to escape.

Who is the first woman to lead the Israelites?

One of the major judges of Israel is a woman named Deborah, who is also a prophetess. Not only does she hear cases that are brought to her for judgment as she "dwells under the palm tree of Deborah," but she is also a military leader. For twenty years, Israel has been subjugated by the Canaanites under their king, Jabin. Deborah clearly decides, prompted by God, that enough is enough. She calls the Israelite general, Barak, and tells him that it is God's will that he wage war on Jabin, and God will grant him victory over Sisera, Jabin's general.

It is evidence of Deborah's power that Barak says, "If thou wilt go with me, then I will go: but if thou wilt not go with me, then I will not go" (Judges 4:8). She's clearly quite a woman.

Who is the woman that Deborah credits with aiding the Israelite victory over the Canaanites?

Despite the fact that they are outnumbered in the battle against Jabin, the Israelites, supported by God, put the Canaanites to flight.

Jabin's general, Sisera, flees on foot and takes refuge in the tent of a woman named Jael, a Kenite. Since the Kenites are not at war with the Canaanites, he thinks he's home free, but Jael has other ideas. She offers Sisera a drink and invites him to rest. Needless to say, after fighting a battle and fleeing on foot, Sisera is ready for a nap, so, after setting Jael to keep watch at the door of the tent, he falls asleep. Big mistake.

As he snoozes, Jael takes a "nail of the tent" (tent peg) and a hammer, and proceeds to nail Sisera to the ground through his temples. As the Bible says, "So he died" (Judges 4:21).

In her song of victory, known as the Song of Deborah, the prophetess gives Jael generous credit for her role in defeating the Canaanites.

The title of Aritha van Herk's second novel, *The Tent Peg* (1981), is taken from this story.

Why did Samson not cut his hair?

Samson is one of the judges of the Israelites during a period when they are oppressed by the Philistines. He is also the original legendary strongman. In the course of his active life he kills a thousand men with the "jawbone of an ass," carries a city gate forty miles, and catches three hundred foxes, ties torches to their tails, and sends them into the Philistines' corn crop to burn it.

The source of his strength is his hair, which he never cuts. Disaster ensues when he succumbs to the charms of a hussy named Delilah, who is in the pay of the Philistines. Three times she asks him the source of his strength, three times he gives her a different answer, three times she binds him in a way she thinks will render him helpless, and three times the Philistines pounce out on him, only to be thrown off. The fourth time Delilah asks, Samson (proving himself less than bright) confesses that his uncut hair is the source of his strength. Delilah cuts off his hair while he sleeps, and the Philistines at last take Samson captive.

The Gideon Bible

On checking into a hotel, most people have found a bible, popularly known as a Gideon Bible, in the room. The name comes directly from the evangelical "parachurch" Christian group that distributes the Bibles: Gideons International.

But why the name? In Judges 6, the Israelites are under the yoke of the Midianites (again). Gideon, a poor man, is busy threshing wheat, but is doing so hidden by a winepress to hide the grain from the Midianites. He seems an unlikely hero. In fact, when the angel of God visits him to say that he is to deliver Israel, even Gideon is astonished. However, he does what God asks of him and the Israelites triumph.

Gideons International chose the name for their organization because Gideon did God's bidding despite any doubts or fears he had himself. This is the spirit that the Gideons want their members to demonstrate, and thus the name.

Gideon's army triumphs over the Midianites by surrounding their camp at night, and then, on God's instructions, blowing on trumpets and breaking ceramic vessels in which were lighted torches. Therefore, the logo of Gideons International contains a two-handled pitcher and a torch.

Formed in Boscobel, Washington, in 1899, Gideons International placed their first Bibles in the rooms of the Superior Hotel, in Superior, Montana, in 1908.

But there's more to it than that. Samson was dedicated to God by his mother at birth. As such, he was forbidden to do a number of things (set out in Numbers 6), including cutting his hair. The hair was the source of his strength because it was part of that bond with God.

Samson and Delilah (1949)

Directed by Cecil B. DeMille, this film is a wonderful example of how Hollywood plays fast and loose with biblical stories. In this version, Samson (Victor Mature) is engaged to a Philistine woman named Semadar (Angela Lansbury, long before *Murder, She Wrote*). At their wedding celebrations, Semadar is killed, and Samson has to flee. The questionably named Saran of Gaza (George Sanders) imposes taxes on the people to get them to give Samson up, and it works. They hand Samson over, but Samson breaks free as he is being taken to the Saran and slaughters the Philistine force that had him captive, using a handy jawbone of an ass that was lying nearby.

Enter Delilah, Semadar's sister (Heddy Lamarr). She suggests to the Saran that she might seduce Samson and get him to reveal the secret of his strength (they kept this part from the Bible). The plan works, but of course she has fallen in love with Samson. Blinded, he is displayed in the temple of Dagon (Hollywood loved those temple scenes) for the pleasure of the Philistines, and Delilah is given a chance to whip him, but instead she guides him to the supporting pillars of the temple. As she flees, Samson brings the building down on the crowd. Having kept about two of the major plot points from the Bible, Hollywood gets its big finish.

The following year, DeMille had a cameo in the 1950 film *Sunset Boulevard*, in a scene where Joan Crawford's character Norma Desmond meets with a director on a film set at Paramount. Amusingly, in DeMille's scene, the movie being shot is *Samson and Delilah*.

What is the first riddle in the Bible?

Samson, to the horror of his mother and father, marries a Philistine woman. At what sounds suspiciously like a stag party, Samson poses a riddle and asks thirty young men to solve it before the seven days of the feast are over. If they do so, he will give them "thirty sheets and thirty change of garments" (Judges 14:12). If they can't give an answer, they owe him the sheets and the garments.

The men go to Samson's wife and beg her to find out the solution to the riddle, and she nags Samson until he tells her. She, of course, tells the young men, who come to Samson with the solution. Samson is not pleased. As he says to them, "If ye had not plowed with my heifer, ye had not found out my riddle." Ouch.

The riddle: "Out of the eater came forth meat, and out of the strong came forth sweetness." The answer is "a lion" and "honey," referring to the fact that Samson had earlier killed a lion and then found a hive of bees in the carcass. You had to be there.

Who is descended from Ruth and Boaz, her second husband?

Ruth and Boaz are the grandparents of Jesse, the father of David, probably the greatest king of Israel. Because their town, Bethlehem, is therefore associated with King David, prophecies in the Old Testament linked Bethlehem with the birth of king who would save Israel. In the New Testament, the gospels of both Matthew and Luke use Jesus' Bethlehem birth as evidence that he is the promised "king," the Messiah.

What does footwear have to do with giving a pledge?

Removing a sandal and giving it to the other party is the sign of a pledge. This what happens in the Book of Ruth, when the kinsman of Ruth's husband relinquishes his rights to Ruth. He removes his sandal and gives it to Boaz, thus sealing the deal.

Ruth, Henry VIII, and Levirate Marriage

The widowed Ruth follows her mother-in-law, Naomi, back to Naomi's home of Bethlehem, and there she meets Naomi's wealthy kinsman Boaz. One thing leads to another and Ruth and Boaz wish to marry, but there is an obstacle in their way: levirate marriage.

In Deuteronomy 25:5, the law says that if a man dies, his brother (or nearest kinsman) must marry his widow and name their first son after his dead brother. The intention of this law is to keep the lineage and name of the dead man alive and his property in the family, but it now presents a problem to Ruth and Boaz, because there is another kinsman that has a more legitimate claim to Ruth. Luckily, the kinsman backs off when reminded of his other responsibilities, such as providing a home for Naomi, and the story has a happy ending.

The waters get muddier in the case of Henry VIII. Henry's first wife, Catherine of Aragon, was initially married to Henry's brother Arthur, but Arthur died, leaving Catherine a widow. Henry stepped up to marry Catherine and keep the connection between England and Spain intact, but he needed special permission from the Pope to do so. This was because, at the time, ecclesiastical law didn't just *not* support levirate marriage, but forbade it on the grounds that it constituted incest. Henry pointed to Deuteronomy to strengthen his case.

The Pope came through, Henry and Catherine were married, and come twenty years go by. At the end of that time, the match had produced only a daughter (Mary, later "Bloody Mary"), and Henry is hankering after an heir. He has also cast his eye on a particularly toothsome lady of the court, Ann Boleyn, who is presumably fertile and attractive to boot.

This is where Henry turns against the concept of levirate marriage. The lack of an heir proves God's displeasure at the "incestuous" marriage, he claims. What is more, he drags up another verse, Leviticus 18:16, that *forbids* a man to marry his brother's wife. The marriage to Catherine must be annulled.

This time the Pope is less pliable (and very aware of Catherine's Spanish Catholic family). And so, to massively simplify matters, Henry VIII starts his own church.

the prophets,
major and minor

What does the word *prophet* mean?

The word *prophet* is taken from Greek, and means "to speak on behalf of another." The biblical prophets, of course, speak on behalf of God, and because they bring news of God's plans, divining the future and warning people what is to come (usually bad) are big items in their skill set.

Were there women prophets?

Though they are certainly less plentiful than male prophets, not only are there women prophets in the Bible, but some of them were among the most revered.

Miriam, Moses' sister, not only stands guard over the infant Moses in the bulrushes, but joins her brothers Moses and Aaron in leading the Israelites out of captivity in Egypt. She is a noted prophetess and a major spiritual leader during the years the Israelites spend wandering in the wilderness. After the parting of the Red Sea, she leads the women in celebration: "And Miriam the prophetess, the sister of Aaron, took a timbrel in her hand; and all the women went out after her with timbrels and with dances." (Exodus 15:20).

As we saw earlier, the prophetess Deborah also acts as a military leader, supporting the Israelite general — who will not go to battle without her — against the Canaanites.

When King Josiah is told that the book of the law predicts Jerusalem's destruction, he sends for the prophetess Huldah (II Kings 22:14 and II Chronicles 34:22). Huldah confirms the coming destruction, but tells Josiah that, because he cared for his people, he will die before it happens. Good news, bad news.

There are other prophetesses referred to, such as the daughters of Philip in the New Testament, as well as Noadiah, Elizabeth, and Anna. These three seem to have had particular influence.

In addition, when the prophet Isaiah decides to procreate, he sleeps with a prophetess, who gives birth to a son.

81

How are the words of the prophet Isaiah represented at the United Nations headquarters in New York?

One of Isaiah's most famous prophecies is a description of a coming day of peace in the "latter days." In Isaiah 2:4, he writes, "They will beat their swords into plowshares, and their spears into pruninghooks: nation shall not lift up sword against nation, neither shall they learn war any more." These words are carved on the Isaiah Wall in Ralph Bunche Park, which is across United Nations Plaza from the U.N. building.

Artwork given by member states is also displayed within the precincts of the U.N. headquarters. In the gardens is a sculpture entitled "Let Us Beat Swords into Plowshares," given to the U.N. in 1959 by the Soviet Union.

What is a plowshare?

The plowshare is the bent cutting or leading edge of a plough. It is extremely sharp and cuts the top layer of the soil.

Isaiah and Handel's Messiah

One of the best-loved musical traditions of the Christmas season, *Messiah*, was actually composed for the theatre and premiered in Dublin during Lent, April 13, 1742.

Although Handel composed the music, the libretto was assembled by Charles Jennens, a patron of the arts, and was planned to tell the Christian story of Christ, the Messiah. The first part of the three-part oratorio deals with many of the prophecies that have been interpreted as pointing to the coming of the Messiah. Jennens drew heavily from the King James Bible for this section (though he also used the Great Bible). One of the main sources of his text was the book of Isaiah, and anyone who has enjoyed a performance of the Messiah will recognize quotes such as, "Behold, a virgin shall conceive, and bear a son, and shall call his name Immanuel"(Isaiah 7:6); "For unto us a son is born, unto us a son is given: and the government shall be upon his shoulder: and his name shall be call be called Wonderful, Counsellor, The mighty God, The everlasting Father, The Prince of Peace" (Isaiah 9:6); and "He is despised and rejected of men; a man of sorrows, and acquainted with grief." It's all Isaiah!

Where do we get the expression "Holier than thou"?

Nowhere is this a good thing. In common usage, of course, it means people who look down on others, thinking themselves superior. In Isaiah 65:5, this is one of the qualities that God sees in his people and that He complains about to Isaiah. In fact, He goes on to say "these are a smoke in my nose." See, He doesn't like those people either.

What does the name *Immanuel* mean?

This name means "God with us." Scholars point out that Isaiah, in prophesying the birth of a child to be called Immanuel, is assuring the king of God's presence and help. In the New Testament, the writers of the gospels take this verse as a prophecy about the coming of Christ, and the name Immanuel is applied to Christ as God on earth.

Does the word *virgin* in the Bible refer to ... well, a virgin?

This is another point over which scholars argue. Isaiah uses the Hebrew word *alma*, and this is what the Bible translates as "virgin." However, in Hebrew, there is no necessary relationship between the word *alma* and virginity. In fact, the word *alma* is often used to indicate a young woman of child-bearing years. The Hebrew word that could mean only "a virgin" is *betulah*.

Where do we get the expression "A lamb to the slaughter"?

This phrase refers to someone who walks into disaster without realizing what has been planned; an innocent. It is particularly useful in times of corporate downsizing.

There are a number of references to animals going "to the slaughter" in the Bible, but perhaps one of the most significant is in Isaiah 53:7: "He was oppressed, and he was afflicted, yet he opened not his mouth: he is brought as a lamb to the slaughter, and as a sheep before her shearers is dumb, so he openeth not his mouth."

In Christian tradition this verse is seen to be a prophecy of the death of Christ, as anyone who has listened to Handel's *Messiah* will know. The allusion to blood sacrifice is clearly intended.

Who is the Bible's first nudist?

Isaiah at one point takes off all his clothes and goes around naked for three years. The explanation given is that he is warning the people around about that the Assyrians will conquer all, and that Judah can't trust Egypt to come to its aid. To deliver this warning, he dresses (or rather, undresses) like a prisoner of war. But *three years*!

Where did we get the expression "No rest for the wicked"?

The literal meaning of this is just what one would think: the wicked have no peace. In fact the biblical verse from which it is taken, Isaiah 57:21, reads: "There is no peace, saith my God, to the wicked."

However, this saying has altered over time. It is now used in a more humorous way, such as when a husband, enjoying the game on television, is rousted out by his wife to cut the grass. "No rest for the wicked," he might exclaim, casting his eyes heavenward.

This change of tone, some suggest, seemed to become more common in the 1930s. Could it be that Harold Gray, creator of Little Orphan Annie, hastened the change in 1933, when he used it as the title for one of his comic strips?

What do we mean by
"put your house in order"?

This is often used to mean the need to wrap up one's affairs before death. As it happens, that's just how it is used in the Bible. In Isaiah 38:1, Hezekiah, king of Judah, is ill, and the prophet Isaiah comes to him to say: "Set thine house in order: for thou shalt die, and not live."

However, there is a happy ending. Hezekiah "turns his face to the wall" and prays to God, who takes pity on him and grants him fifteen more years of life. Interestingly, turning one's face to the wall has come to refer to someone giving up on life, rather than buying themselves more time.

How does Isaiah die?

No one knows for sure, but traditionally he is thought to have been sawn in two by the wicked King Manasseh, son of King Hezekiah.

Where do we get the expression "A drop in the bucket"?

This used to describe something that is totally minuscule in comparison to the whole, or insignificant, especially in view of the larger picture. It is taken from Isaiah 40:15, where the prophet Isaiah reminds King Hezekiah of the power of God: "Behold, the nations are as a drop of a bucket [to God]."

Who is the Bible's most noted depressive?

The prophet Jeremiah is such a downer, he is known as the "Weeping Prophet." To be fair, he lived during the destruction of Jerusalem by the Babylonians, and no one listened to his warnings. It's enough to depress a prophet.

Why do we ask, "Can a leopard change its spots?"

This is a question about whether someone can change their essential nature. It is usually used when someone who has always acted one way suddenly starts acting another, and the implied answer is "No." This is the way that cheery prophet Jeremiah used it (Jeremiah 13:23) when foretelling the punishment of God upon the people for their sinful ways.

What do we mean by "sour grapes"?

Both Jeremiah and the prophet Ezekiel, writing in a difficult time, quote a proverb that was seemingly common in their day: "The fathers have

"Dem Dry Bones"

This well-known traditional spiritual is based on Ezekiel 37, in which the prophet has a vision of a valley of dry bones. God instructs him to prophesy that the bones will live and, before his eyes, the bones come together to create skeletons, and then grow muscles, tendons, and flesh. Despite the gruesome nature of the vision, it is meant to convey a message of hope that the Israelites, scattered and in exile, will eventually be brought back together and their nation will live again. It is understandable that this theme would appeal to those who are also captive and in slavery.

Although the song is traditional, the melody was written by the African-American songwriter James Weldon Johnson.

Because the verses run through the bones of the body (inaccurately) — "Toe bone connected to the foot bone, / Foot bone connected to the heel bone, / The heel bone connected to the ankle bone," and so on — the song was allegedly used to teach anatomy to children. The Simpsons episode "Homer's Triple Bypass," in which the doctor tries to jog his memory of anatomy in the middle of an operation by singing this song, echoes this usage.

The song has been played by a variety of musicians over the years, including, among many others, Fats Waller, The Delta Rhythm Boys, The Four Lads, the Mills Brothers, and Rosemary Clooney. Even The Kinks used the chorus in their own song "Skin and Bone" (1971).

Fans of the cult hit The Prisoner will remember that the song features prominently in the final episode, "Fall Out," and it is sung by Peter O'Toole in the film The Ruling Class (1972).

eaten sour grapes, and the children's teeth are set on edge" (Jeremiah 31: 29 and Ezekiel 18:2). The meaning here is that the suffering of the people is a result of the mistakes or sins of previous generations.

Although many point to this as the source of our own use of "sour grapes," the meaning is quite different. Today we use the expression when someone has lost something they wanted, and so disparage it, pretend that they didn't want it at all. It is much more likely that this usage comes from Aesop's fable of "The Fox and the Grapes."

Who does God order to marry a prostitute?

Symbolism is very important in the Bible, and in the lives of the prophets. The prophet Hosea may have been puzzled when God told him to marry a prostitute named Gomer (yeah, really). He would have been within his rights to be ticked off when Gomer was unfaithful to him. However, God meant this to symbolize the "unfaithfulness" of Israel towards God and his commandments.

What is the shortest book in the Hebrew Bible?

The book of Obadiah is the shortest at a brisk twenty-one verses.

What was it that swallowed Jonah?

If you said Jonah was swallowed by a whale, you are certainly in line with popular tradition but you're not absolutely correct, though we can agree that Jonah was swallowed by a big fish. In fact, the phrase used in Hebrew is *dag gadol*, which translates exactly as "big fish." The Hebrew language, in fact, has only one word for water creatures, *dag*, since the Israelites were not noticeably nautical.

Which prophet was instrumental in the magi finding Jesus?

When the magi come to the court of King Herod looking for the "King of the Jews," the wise men of the court consult their writings. In the book of the prophet Micah, they find the verse "But thou Bethlehem Ephratah, though thou be little among the thousands of Judah, yet out of thee shall he come forth unto me that is to be ruler in Israel" (Micah 5:2). That's good enough for the magi.

exile and homecoming: Ezra, Nehemiah, Esther, and Daniel

Who are the first in the Bible
to choose vegetarianism?

In the sixth century B.C.E., the Israelites find themselves exiled to Babylon. Since many of those carried off by the Babylonians are from the educated class, King Nebuchadnezzar decides that he can use some of the young men in his service in the palace. Four of those chosen for this "privilege" are Daniel and his three buddies, Shadrach, Meshach, and Abednego. One snag is that, during their training, they are expected to live and eat like their Babylonian compatriots.

The Babylonians don't observe the same dietary laws as the Israelites, and the meat and wine that Daniel and his friends are expected to eat is far from kosher, so they request that they be allowed to drink water and eat lentils (also known as "pulses"). At first there is resistance to this, since the king has no interest in pale, droopy servants. However, Daniel proposes a ten-day trial, and at the end of that time he and his friends are even more fit and peppy than all the other trainees. They get their water and pulses. Yum.

Why do we speak of someone having "feet of clay"?

An esteemed figure who turns out to be flawed is said to have "feet of clay." The expression comes from Daniel 2, in which Daniel interprets a dream of King Nebuchadnezzar (Daniel, like Joseph, has the gift of dream interpretation). The king has dreamed of a mighty statue of precious metals: its head is gold, its body is silver and bronze, but its feet are of clay and iron. When a stone hits the feet, they crumble, breaking the statue in pieces. Daniel interprets this as foretelling the break-up of powerful empires. Although in Daniel the interpretation was intensely political, to the average person the moral is that no matter how great and powerful something or someone may be, a weak foundation will lead to destruction.

Who was thrown into the "fiery furnace"?

In Daniel 3, Nebuchadnezzar sets up a ninety-foot-tall gold statue and orders that the people all worship it. Three of Daniel's friends, Shadrach, Meshach, and Abednego, refuse to worship this idol and are thrown into a "fiery furnace" to be burnt to cinders. So hot is the furnace that the men who are doing the throwing are struck dead by the heat.

But not the three friends. What is more, when Nebuchadnezzar looks into the furnace, he sees four men walking around in the middle of the flames, and "the form of the fourth is like the Son of God."

The king orders them to be taken out of the furnace, and they walk out without the slightest mark of burning on them or their clothes. Nebuchadnezzar therefore orders that no one can say anything bad about the god of Shadrach, Meshach, and Abednego, on pain of death and of having their homes reduced to a "dung heap."

This story has entered our culture. It is alluded to in a hymn sung regularly in the Eastern Orthodox Church, and "The Burning Fiery Furnace" is one of the three parables in Benjamin Britten's *Parables for Church Performance*. "The Fourth Man in the Fire" is a song by Johnny Cash, the Beastie Boys sang "Shadrach" in 1989, and Sly and the Family Stone sing the names of the three friends over and over in their song "Loose Booty." A character in Toni Morrison's *Sula* is named Shadrack, who is seen as a prophet.

Where did the expression "The writing is on the wall" come from?

This is used to mean that something (usually interpreted as something undesirable) is about to take place, and the signs are clear. It comes from the story of another occasion when Daniel was called on to interpret a dream.

In Daniel 5, Belshazzar, son of Nebuchadnezzar, is hosting a wing-ding of a party. He and his sons and wives and concubines are eating and drinking and making merry, using the gold and silver vessels that

TOP 10 OCCUPATIONS IN BIBLICAL TIMES

Since the Bible covers around two thousand years of history, the occupations varied over time as the population made the transition from nomadic herders to settled agriculturists. By the time of the New Testament, most people worked in villages or the surrounding farmlands.

1   **Farmer:** This was the largest employer in biblical times, as food was necessary for the Israelites' survival, and, since farming was done manually, it required a very large labour force. Farmers supplied the population with olives for olive oil, grapes for wine, wheat and barley for flour, lentils, peas, dates (an important early source of sugar), and figs.

2.   **Shepherd:** Shepherds generally did not own the flock, but took care of the animals for their owner. The shepherd had to ensure the flock had sufficient food and water and had to protect the flock from predators (including wolves, hyenas, jackals, lions, and bears) and thieves. Should an animal be lost, the shepherd had to pay the owner for the cost of the animal, a large incentive indeed to take care of the flock.

3.   **Builder:** During the centuries covered by the Bible, the population moved to villages with buildings of various types, so builders were required for houses, shops, temples, and eventually palaces and fortresses.

4.   **Weaver:** People needed clothing to wear, and that is where weavers came in. Clothing production was predominantly handled by women. The fabrics were made of wool — harvested from sheep in the spring — and of goat hair and flax. Various vegetable dyes were used to add some colour to the clothing.

5.   **Fisherman:** Since the Philistines controlled the coastal areas, this occupation was only significant near large inland bodies of water such as the Sea of Galilee. Fishermen and the sea do however figure prominently in the stories of the New Testament: four of the apostles were fishermen, and Jesus' miracles included walking on the water, feeding 5,000 people with two fish (and seven loaves of bread), and calming the stormy water when out in a boat.

6.   **Scribe:** Since the law was of paramount importance to the Israelites, it was necessary to have people employed in studying and interpreting the law. Initially this was handled by the priests, but over time a new class of worker arose to take over this function. These were the scribes, equivalent to today's lawyers. Eventually the scribes became an extremely influential group in the Israeli society.

7.   **Government Worker:** As the Israelites made the transition from a nomadic to a more settled lifestyle, the tribal system, they required tribal clerks and tax collectors (the profession of one of the apostles) as leaders.

8.   **Soldier:** Initially the Israelites, following their nomadic tradition, had no permanent army, but each tribe of Israel provided a militia force when

> necessary. After King Saul, the militia was discarded in favour of the more usual army model used by their enemies. The soldiers themselves comprised four groups based on the weapon they used: slings (as David used with Goliath), bows, swords/axes/maces, and spears/javelins. Every male member of the tribes of Israel over twenty years old was expected to perform military service. It is interesting to note that, as the Israeli army was small compared to its aggressive neighbours, the army tended to engage in more guerrilla tactics than outright campaigns.
>
> 9. **Miller:** An important part of the food business, this was initially done by women at home as part of a normal list of chores, but with larger villages and cities it became an important industry in itself.
>
> 10 **Potter:** Making pottery is one of the world's oldest crafts, with the oldest examples made by the ancient Egyptians. In biblical times, the making of various earthenware containers was a thriving industry, and Jerusalem in fact had its own ceramics district. Pottery was mainly used for cooking, for storing liquids (oil, wine, water), grains, and fruits.

Nebuchadnezzar "liberated" from the Temple in Jerusalem. While they are doing this, the fingers of a man's hand appear and write on the wall. What's that about?

The queen remembers that Daniel has gifts in this area, and he is called on to interpret. As may be expected, the news is not good for a king who has defiled the holy vessels from Jerusalem. Daniel interprets the phrase that has been written — "*Mene, mene, tekel, uparsin*" — to mean that the kingdom will be divided between the Medes and Persians. To get the ball rolling, the Persians take over Babylon that very night, and kill Belshazzar.

Why do we refer to someone facing an intimidating experience as "Daniel in the lions' den"?

King Darius of Persia, who is now in charge in Babylon, promotes Daniel to a high position in court. Unfortunately, some of the other officials are jealous of Daniel and also know of his religious beliefs. They convince the king to command that, for a month, no one can ask anything of another god or — or human — other than Darius himself.

Quickies
Did you know ...
- that the expression "one's days are numbered" comes from the same source as "the writing is on the wall" — Daniel's encounter with Belshazzar? As Daniel says in his prediction of Belshazzar's downfall, "God has numbered they kingdom, and finished it" (Daniel 5:26).

Daniel, Shakespeare, and Rumpole of the Bailey
Fans of John Mortimer's irascible lawyer, Rumpole of the Bailey, will no doubt be familiar with his love of referencing Shakespeare. He gives his esteemed female colleague, Phyllida Erskine-Brown, the name of "Portia" after Portia in *The Merchant of Venice* (who disguises herself as a law clerk to argue a case and save her beloved Bassanio). When he hears a legal decision he likes, he echoes Shylock's words, "A Daniel come to judgment! Yea, a Daniel."

But where did Shakespeare get this expression? It is very probable that he was alluding to the biblical Daniel. As the king Belshazzar said (Daniel 5:14), when he called Daniel to interpret the mysterious writing on the wall (see above), "excellent wisdom is found in thee."

Daniel cannot deny God, and he continues to pray three times a day, facing Jerusalem. In the way of such sneaks, the jealous officials immediately scuttle off to Darius and inform on him.

Darius is upset, since he quite likes Daniel, but an edict is an edict. Into the lions' den goes Daniel, and the king has a sleepless night, imagining the carnage taking place.

God, however, is looking out for the faithful Daniel, and has prevented the lions from attacking him. Come the morning, Darius finds Daniel alive and well. To celebrate, he orders the jealous officials and their families thrown into the lions' den, and the lions, denied their bedtime snack the night before, make short work of them.

What is Esther's connection with Haddassah, the Jewish volunteer women's organization?

In the book of Esther, it is the fifth century B.C.E. and the Persian king Ahasueris (most likely Xerxes) rules over Babylon, and those Jews who have not returned to their homeland are working hard to avoid being assimilated. Many of them have Babylonian names, but also keep their Hebrew names. The name Esther is derived from the Babylonian fertility goddess, Ishtar, but Esther's Hebrew name is Haddassah.

As her story opens, the king is furious at his wife, Vashti, for defying him, and determines to find a new wife. He sets up an elaborate contest to try out the virgins of the kingdom, and Esther, who has to this point concealed her Jewish roots, wins his favour and becomes queen.

Meanwhile, her cousin Mordecai has been hanging around the palace to keep an eye on her. Unfortunately, Haman, a top palace official, is insulted that Mordecai the Jew will not bow to him, and hatches a plot to destroy him. Not naming the Jews specifically, he convinces the king to sign an edict to destroy "a certain people" who are undermining the king's law, and the king gives Haman the authority to carry out the persecution. Haman casts dice, "purim," to decide on which month to eliminate the Jews, and settles on the thirteenth day of the twelfth month (this becomes important later).

Mordecai pleads with Esther to intervene for her people, and, despite her fear of approaching the king without being invited, Esther agrees. She builds up to her big request. First she invites the king and Haman to dinner, and there the charmed king grants her a wish. She asks for another dinner with the same guests the next day. Then, at the second dinner, she asks that she and her people be spared. The king is shocked. "Who would threaten you?" he asks, and Esther fingers Haman, confessing to the king her relationship to Mordecai. Haman is summarily hanged on the gallows he had prepared for Mordecai, but the king cannot undo an edict that has been issued.

Instead, the king allows Mordecai to issue another proclamation, urging the Jews to defend themselves on the day Haman set for their destruction and encouraging other people to help. The Jews triumph and are saved.

On the fourteenth and fifteenth of the twelfth month, the Jews celebrate their triumph and resolve to celebrate it every year thereafter. This is the Jewish celebration of Purim, which is still celebrated on the fifteenth day of the Jewish month of Adar.

Hadassah was established by Henrietta Szold and the Daughters of Zion in New York City in 1912. Because the founders' meeting took place at the same time as the holiday of Purim, the group took Esther's Hebrew name, Hadassah.

What book of the Bible never mentions God?

Esther not only doesn't mention God, but doesn't record any religious practices. Because of this, the compilers of the Bible hesitated over the inclusion of Esther.

When was the Second Temple in Jerusalem built?

Quickies
Did you know ...
• that Ezra 7:21 contains every letter of the alphabet except *j*?

In 539 B.C.E., Cyrus the Great of Persia allows those Jews who wish to do so to return to their homeland. Resettling takes quite a bit of work, however, and although the returnees lay the (smaller) foundation of a new temple (Ezra 5:16), it takes the nagging of the prophets Haggai and Zechariah, and the funding of the new Persian king, Darius, to get the job done. It isn't until 515 B.C.E. that the Second Temple is dedicated.

writings, poetry, and songs: Job, Psalms, Proverbs, Ecclesiastes, Song of Songs

What is meant by the word *proverb*?

Proverb is the translation of the Hebrew word *mashal*, which means "to rule" or "to govern." A proverb is a rule or a saying that helps us to run, or govern, our lives.

Who wrote the book of Proverbs?

This is another case of tradition versus what can actually be proved. Tradition says that Solomon wrote Proverbs, and that is an appealing thought, given Solomon's reputation for wisdom and the fact that he is reported to have written some three thousand proverbs. Some of the chapters actually begin with a claim that they are the work of Solomon. For instance, the first words in Proverbs 1:1 are, "The proverbs of Soloman the son of David, king of Israel." At the same time, other proverbs are attributed to other figures, none of them traceable.

It seems that Proverbs, like the Bible itself, is a compilation of works, in this case a collection of wise sayings.

What does Proverbs have to do with the Humane Society?

In direct contradiction of those who argue that concern for animals is a modern affectation, Proverbs 12:10 states, "A righteous man regardeth the life of his beast: but the tender mercies of the wicked are cruel."

Where do we get the expression "Pride goes before a fall"?

This is taken from Proverbs 16:18: "Pride goeth before destruction, and an haughty spirit before a fall." In Proverbs it means just what it means today: those who are filled with pride and self-satisfaction will fail.

Where does it say, "Spare the rod and spoil the child"?

It doesn't say exactly that in the Bible, but that's where we get the expression. Proverbs 13:24 reads, "He that spareth his rod, hateth his son: but he that loveth him chasteneth him betimes." Interestingly, this seems to have been a piece of general wisdom in the ancient world. Passages from both Proverbs and Ecclesiastes bear a striking resemblance to *The Words of Ahiqar*, supposedly written by an official in the Assyrian court. There the similar passage reads, "withhold not the rod from your son, or else you will not be able to save him." It seems the ancient jury on permissive parenting is in.

What does the name Satan mean?

The Hebrew name Satan actually means "the adversary," and that's certainly the role he plays in the Book of Job, standing as Job's adversary in the court of heaven. In Greek, the word "adversary" is *diabolos*, from which we get "devil." Please note, there is not a cloven hoof or a forked tail on Satan in the entire Bible.

Another name for Satan is Beezebul, or "Prince Baal." Our more familiar Beelzebub is a pun on Beezebul, and its English translation is "Lord of the Flies."

William Golding chose this as a title for his 1954 novel about the innate evil in human nature.

> **Quickies**
> *Did you know ...*
> • that the 2009 film *A Serious Man* by the Coen brothers is a modern retelling of the Book of Job?

What is meant by a "Job's comforter"?

Job is an upright and virtuous man, but he has had terrible misfortune piled on him. His donkeys, oxen, and camels have been stolen, his sheep burned in a fire, his servants have been slain, and his ten children have been killed in the collapse of the house they were in. In addition, he has broken out in painful boils all over his body. From a wealthy and respected man, he has been reduced to a suffering wretch, sitting on a pile of ashes.

Three of his friends come around to be with him, but after sitting silently and observing his terrible pain, they start trying to come up with an explanation for his misfortune. He must have sinned somehow, so that God is punishing him, they insist.

> **Quickies**
> *Did you know ...*
> • that the Behemoth and the Leviathan mentioned in Job are thought by some scholars to represent the hippopotamus and the crocodile.

Job knows he is innocent, so their intervention is less than useless; it is an added pain.

A Job's comforter has come to mean someone who, though attempting to comfort someone, only succeeds in making them feel worse.

Where do we get the expression "By the skin of your teeth"?

This means "by a narrow margin" and is often used to describe a close call of some sort. In the Bible, the phrase appears in Job 19:20, as Job enumerates his many losses: "My bone cleaveth to my skin, and I am escaped with the skin of my teeth." Since teeth don't have skin, he seems to be saying that he has escaped with nothing. Note: Job says "with," not "by," but the Revised Standard Version of the Bible translates the phrase as "*by* the skin of my teeth," suggesting that the modern usage is correct.

What does the word *vanity* mean in Ecclesiastes?

The book of Ecclesiastes is not exactly a million laughs, but then it does set out to discover meaning in life, which is a serious study.

It wastes no time in getting down to business. In the second verse (Ecclesiastes 1:2) it sets the tone with the well-known line, "Vanity of vanities; all is vanity." But what does vanity mean? It doesn't mean "I think I'm special" in the way it does today.

The Hebrew word used is *hevel*, which literally means breath or vapour, but because it is used as a metaphor, it could be — and is — translated to indicate general futility. Various translators have rendered it as "futile," "meaningless," "senseless," and "pointless."

Break out the party hats.

Where do we get the expression "Nothing new under the sun"?

This world-weary expression is taken from Ecclesiastes 1:9: "and there is no new thing under the sun." The meaning is clear, and exactly what one might expect from a writer who thinks everything is futile.

Where does it say, "Eat, drink, and be merry"?

On the face of things, it's pretty clear what this means. However, the phrase comes from Ecclesiastes (8:15), the same book that reminds us that "all is vanity." So, before you break out the lager, remember that the common continuation of the saying — "for tomorrow you may die" — is more in keeping with the spirit of Ecclesiastes.

> **Quickies**
> *Did you know ...*
> • that the command "cast your bread upon the waters," which is often thought to call for charity (or even prayerful investing), may refer to beer-making. This may just be another way of saying, "Eat, drink, and be merry [for tomorrow you may die]."

Where do we get the expression "A fly in the ointment"?

This describes a small flaw or glitch that manages to spoil the entire thing. It is taken from Ecclesiastes 10:1, where a touch of folly is said to spoil a reputation for wisdom. Ointment, by the way, refers to perfume, not your favourite antibiotic cream.

To Every Thing There Is a Season

This very well-known expression, meaning that there is a right time for everything, comes from Ecclesiastes 3 and probably owes much of its familiarity to folk artist Pete Seeger, who set the verse to music in 1959.

"To Everything There Is a Season" was released by both the Limeliters and by Pete Seeger himself in 1962. In 1963, Judy Collins recorded the song, re-titling it "Turn! Turn! Turn! (to Everything There is a Season)." This is the title that was used by The Byrds when they recorded it in 1965. If, as tradition has it, King Solomon wrote Ecclesiastes (though tradition has him writing just about everything), this would make him the oldest songwriter with a number-one pop hit. Seeger donated 45 percent of his royalties to Israeli Committee Against House Demolitions, keeping 55 percent because, as he pointed out, as well as the music, "I did write six words."

What is the advice Ecclesiastes gives to publishers?

TOP 10 MOST MENTIONED NAMES

1. David: 1,139 times
2. Jesus: 983
3. Moses: 848
4. Saul: 425
5. Jacob: 345
6. Aaron: 350
7. Solomon: 306
8. Abraham: 250
9. Joseph: 250
10. Joshua: 216

The name *Judah* appears 817 times, but, although he was one of Jesus' ancestors, the name was not included in the list because it also appears as the name of a tribe and a kingdom. Also, *God* appears 4,473 times, and the *Lord* appears 7,970 times. The lowly *Satan* appears only 56 times.

Ecclesiastes 12:12 reads, in part, "Of making many books there is no end; and much study is a weariness of the flesh." Amen.

Why is the "Song of Songs" also called the "Song of Solomon"?

This ancient love poem is known as the "Song of Songs," "the Song of Solomon," "Solomon's Song," or as "Canticles." The name is a form of superlative, meaning this is the best of all the songs, while "Canticles" is the short form of the Latin, *Canticum Canticorum*. The connection with Solomon comes from the first verse, "The song of songs, which is

Solomon's," but his authorship is by no means certain, even if he is said to have written 1,005 songs.

What is an orphaned psalm?

Many of the hymns of praise recorded in Psalms have a note on them, saying when they were written or who is supposed to have composed them. Many of them are attributed to King David, especially because of his close identification with music, and specifically the lyre. Of the 150 Psalms, only 34 have no notation, and are referred to as "orphaned psalms." Of course, scholars still debate the accuracy of the notations on the others.

Where do we get the expression "The apple of my eye"?

Literally, this means the very centre of the eye, but symbolically it means something or someone that is valued, and usually loved, more than any other.

Given the prevalence of eye imagery in many cultures, it is no surprise to find it loaded with significance. The expression is used more than once in the Bible, but perhaps the best known is Psalms 17:8: "Keep me as the apple of the eye, hide me under the shadow of thy wings."

What Psalm did Jesus quote on the cross?

According to Matthew 27:46: "And about the ninth hour, Jesus cried with a loud voice, saying, Eli, Eli, lama sabachthani? that is to say, My God, my God, why has thou forsaken me?" This is a direct quote from the lament in Psalm 22.

Where do we get the expression
"From strength to strength"?

This means to move from one success to another. In Psalms 84:7, the psalmist is describing the lives of the righteous. "They go from strength to strength, every one of them in Zion appeareth before God."

What were the most common instruments
used in the Bible?

In its injunction to praise God, Psalm 150 presents a handy list of common instruments. It mentions trumpets, harps, tambourines, strings, pipes, and cymbals. Judging from this and other sources, drums and tambourines seem to predominate (remember Miriam and her timbrel, or hand drum?), while the lyre and flute are also plentiful. Interestingly, the percussion instruments seem to be used by women, while lyres are played by men, the opposite of present-day expectations.

Which psalm inspired Martin Luther's famous hymn
"A Mighty Fortress Is Our God"?

This is probably the most famous of Martin Luther's hymns. Written between 1527 and 1529, it was first translated into English from German by Myles Coverdale (of the Coverdale Bible) in 1539. Since then some seventy English translations have been done, the most popular being Frederick J. Hedge's 1853 translation: "A mighty fortress is our God / a bulwark never failing."

It is said that King Gustavus of Sweden played it as a battle hymn for his forces in the Thirty Years War, and it was sung at the funeral of President Dwight Eisenhower.

The words are a paraphrase by Luther of Psalm 46.

Where do we get the expression "At one's wits' end"?

This expression, meaning that one is out of ideas and unable to think of a solution, is taken from Psalms 107:27: "They reel to and fro, and stagger like a drunken man, and are at their wit's end." Perhaps this is a clue to why they are at their wits' end.

By the Rivers of Babylon

"By the rivers of Babylon, there we sat down, yea, we wept, when we remembered Zion" (Psalm 137:1).

One of the best-known of the psalms, Psalm 137 clearly refers to the exile of the Jewish people in Babylon — making it clear that all the writings in Psalms can not be dated to the same period and that David did not write them all. The rivers referred to are the Euphrates and its tributaries.

It has been set to music by, or has influenced, a wide variety of musicians, including Palestrina, Verdi (for whom it inspired the slave chorus from *Nabucco*), William Walton, as well as Brent Dowe and Trevor McNaughton of The Melodians. McNaughton and Dowe's "Rivers of Babylon" (1972) was heard in the soundtrack of the movie *The Harder They Fall*, but is probably better known for Boney M's 1978 cover version. "Babylon" was the last track on Don McLean's 1971 album, *American Pie*.

The title of William Faulkner's 1939 novel, *If I Forget Thee Jerusalem*, is taken from Verse 5, and Stephen Vincent Benet entitled a 1937 short story "By the Waters of Babylon." Other authors have played with the words of the Psalm. In *The Waste Land*, T.S. Eliot writes, "By the waters of Leman [Lake Geneva] I sat down and wept," while Elizabeth Smart's 1945 novel in prose poetry is entitled *By Grand Central Station I Sat Down and Wept*.

Clearly the Psalms continue to inspire.

THE
NEW TESTAMENT

the life of Jesus: Matthew, Mark, Luke, and John

Did Matthew, Mark, Luke, and John actually write the gospels?

That hasn't been definitely established. These names were certainly not attached to the original writings, but they were added early in the days of the Church, based on internal evidence and early church beliefs about who wrote them. All the books deal with much of the same material — the life of Christ — but from slightly different angles.

Did Matthew, Mark, Luke, and John know Jesus personally?

Matthew and John were among Jesus's inner circle of twelve disciples. Luke and Mark were not among this group, but were friends of the apostle Paul, who was immensely influential in the early church. In addition, there is a belief that Mark did know Jesus, and was present when Jesus was arrested.

What are the symbols of Matthew, Mark, Luke, and John?

Christian tradition for centuries has used four symbols to represent the "four evangelists." These symbols are taken from the vision of the prophet Ezekiel, in which he sees four heavenly creatures with four faces each: "As for the likeness of their faces, they four had the face of a man, and the face of a lion, on the right side: and they four had the face of an ox on the left side; they four also had the face of an eagle" (Ezekiel 1:10).

In Christian iconography Matthew is represented by the figure of a man (or angel), Mark by a lion, Luke by an ox, and John by an eagle. These symbols of the evangelists are so widespread in Western art that a knowledge of the symbolism is essential to the study of art and sculpture.

What does the word *gospel* mean?

The actual source of this word is the Greek work *euangelion*. What's the connection? *Euangelion* means "good news," which is how the early Christian writers viewed the story of Jesus. This is the source of the words *evangelist* and *evangelism*, referring to the spreader and the spreading of the "good news."

The Anglo-Saxon for "good news" is *god-spell*, and that has become "gospel."

Godspell

This upbeat off-Broadway and Broadway hit, which uses the ancient form of "gospel" for its title, started life as the master's thesis of John-Michael Trebelak, and was first performed at Carnegie Mellon University. The show traced the arc of Jesus's life from his baptism by John to his death, and ends in a joyful finale. Trebelak based his work on the gospels of Matthew and Luke and, when members of the college's music department wrote songs for it, they borrowed heavily from the *Episcopal Hymnal* for the lyrics. When the show moved to New York in 1971 for a short run at an experimental theatre, it caught the eye of producers James Beruh and Edgar Lansbury (Angela Lansbury's brother), who hired Stephen Schwartz to write new songs. Schwartz wrote new lyrics, but kept material from the *Episcopal Hymnal*.

Godspell became one of the longest-running off-Broadway productions and then moved to Broadway in 1976, where it ran for over a year.

Meanwhile, the show was also being performed in cities around the world. The Toronto production helped change the face of the city's theatre scene and launch the careers of such present-day household names as Gilda Radner, Martin Short, Eugene Levy, Andrea Martin, and Dave Thomas. *Godspell* was also made into a film in 1973.

It has now permeated our culture. For instance, Ford Prefect in *The Hitchhiker's Guide to the Galaxy* keeps a copy of the script of *Godspell* at hand in order to make people think he's an actor.

Who is the famous ancestor of Mary and Joseph?

According to the gospels, Mary and Joseph are said to descend from King David. This is important, since at the time of Jesus's birth Israel was under the rule of Rome, and many Jews were longing for a "king" to deliver them.

Where do the names *Messiah* and *Christ* come from?

Messiah is derived from a Hebrew word meaning "anointed one," and refers to the king that the Jews were expecting. The Greek version is *Christos*, from which we get *Christ*.

Was Jesus really born in a cattle shed?

Debate swirls around this one. The common Christmas picture has Mary and Joseph out in what seems to be a stable, because it is said that Mary laid the infant Jesus in a "manger," and a manger is a trough for feeding animals.

However, there is no evidence in the gospels that this is actually what happened. The word that is translated as "inn," is the Greek *kataluma*, which has a number of meanings. It can also mean the guest room of a house. (In fact, the only other time the word is used in the New Testament, it refers to the upper room where Jesus and his disciples celebrate the Last Supper.) Because of this, and because Mary and Joseph are returning to their hometown, some scholars suggest that it meant the guest room in a family home, which was crowded with other family members due to the census.

There is, by the way, also no friendly innkeeper who ushers the young couple into the barn. He's a later addition.

What is a feeding trough doing in a house? In the ancient world, animals were often kept inside homes. Ground-floor rooms would house animals, tools, animal feed — and mangers. The family would sleep on the second floor. This was a very practical arrangement. The animals were indoors and protected from weather and thieves, while the sleeping homeowners benefitted from the body heat of the animals and ready access to milk and other necessities.

So, according to many scholars, we can scratch the inn, the innkeeper, and

Quickies

Did you know ...

- that the scene in which Gabriel announces to Mary that she is to bear the son of God — the Annunciation — appears only in the gospel of Luke.

112

the barn, and place Mary and Joseph in the ground-floor of an overcrowded family home.

Today, the Church of the Nativity in Bethlehem marks the supposed site of the birth — be it home or stable.

> **Quickies**
>
> *Did you know ...*
> - that the population of the world at the time of Christ is estimated at 200 million?

What year was Jesus born?

More controversy. The present calculation of B.C.E. and C.E. was based on a sixth-century calculation, which is now thought to have been a few years off.

The census that takes Mary and Joseph to Bethlehem is recorded as occurring in 6 B.C.E. Matthew and Luke both place the birth during the reign of Herod the Great, and Herod died in 4 B.C.E. As a further complication, Herod's command to kill all boys under two years of age suggests that Jesus might have been as old as two when the order was given.

As a result of all this, most scholars think that Jesus was born around 6 or 5 B.C.E.

Was Jesus actually born on December 25?

No one knows what time of the year Jesus was born, and the New Testament isn't telling.

The choice of December 25 came later, after Christianity had spread and had been exposed to other religious traditions. The early Christians were very adept at using these traditions and fitting them into a Christian context. This made the early church stand out less, and it also made it easier for foreign converts to adapt.

Scholars think that the early church settled on December 25 to commemorate the birth of Christ because that was the date of the Roman festival of Saturnalia. Saturnalia marked the winter solstice, when the days began lengthening and the new life of spring was near, so the symbolism worked well. While the Romans were celebrating the return of the sun, the Christians were celebrating the birth of the Son.

Who were the three wise men?

Only one of the gospels — Matthew — mentions the wise men, and it calls them only "wise men from the east." They themselves tell Herod that they are following a star. Because of this, the majority opinion among scholars seems to be that they were Zoroastrian priests from Babylon, which was the centre of astrology. There they might also have encountered Judaism. They are often also referred to as the *Magi*, since this title is related to the priestly caste of Zorastrianism (founded by Zoroaster in the sixth century B.C.E.).

There is no evidence that there were three of them. Because three gifts — gold, frankincense, and myrrh — are mentioned, it has been traditional to assume there were three wise men. There may have been a battalion. The gifts, by the way, were the sort of tribute one would present to a king.

There is also no reason to think that the wise men were there in the manger with the shepherds. Matthew and Luke, who record the nativity story, have conflicting agendas. Luke wishes to portray Jesus as a man of the people, while Matthew wishes to emphasize Jesus's kingship. Therefore Luke brings in the lowly shepherds, while Matthew emphasizes the visit of the wise men who wish to pay tribute to a king. Nowhere are they present at the same time.

Western Christian tradition has named the wise men Balthazar, Caspar, and Melchior, but this has nothing to do with the Bible. These names come from a Greek manuscript, probably written in Alexandria circa 500 C.E.

Why did King Herod have mother-in-law issues?

Although this doesn't appear in the Bible, it does shed some light on Herod's biblical shenanigans.

Herod married Mariamne, a princess of the Hasmoneans, a ruling Jewish family in Israel. The plan was that this would legitimize his reign. However, suspecting her of adultery, Herod — ever the hothead — had Mariamne killed.

Understandably, Mariamne's mother took offence and entered into a plot with Cleopatra of Egypt (she was a busy lady) to unseat Herod and put one of her grandsons on the throne.

So Herod killed her too.

Quickies
Did you know ...
- that myrrh is an anointing oil, used at the crowning of kings. It is also considered by the Eastern Orthodox Church to be a holy oil, used when confirming someone into the church or anointing the dying. Because of this, receiving either sacrament is known as "receiving the Myrrh."

Quickies
Did you know ...
- that "The Gift of the Magi" is probably the best-known of the short stories of writer O. Henry.

We Three Kings of Orient Are

This well-known American carol was written in 1857 by Reverand John Henry Hopkins, reportedly for a Christmas pageant at the General Theological Seminary in New York City.

Reverand Hopkins, who one presumes had theological training, works into his verses the spiritual meaning of the gifts of the wise men.

Gold symbolizes kingship: "Gold I bring to crown him again / King forever, ceasing never / Over us all to reign."

Frankincense (an incense) symbolizes priesthood: "Frankincense to offer have I / Incense owns a deity nigh / Prayer and praising, all men raising / Worship him God most high."

Myrrh (an embalming oil), symbolizes death: "Myrrh is mine, its bitter perfume Breathes of life of gathering gloom / Sorrowing, sighing, bleeding, dying / Sealed in the stone-cold tomb.

What is Jesus's relationship to John the Baptist?

John the Baptist is the son of Zechariah and Elizabeth, and Elizabeth is Mary's cousin. Therefore, John and Jesus are second cousins.

After the Annunciation, Mary goes to visit Elizabeth. Elizabeth is six months pregnant with John, and when she hears Mary's greeting, "the babe leaped in her womb"(Luke 1:44). This prefigures John's role as the one who is to prepare the way for Jesus.

What did John the Baptist eat?

John the Baptist may have been holy, but he also sounds a bit like the original "hippy." As Matthew 3:4 tells it, he "had his raiment of camel's hair, and a leathern girdle about his loins, and his meat was locusts and wild honey."

Where do we get the expression "Separate the wheat from the chaff"?

This means separating important things from the unimportant and is an agricultural image, referring to the separation of the valuable kernel of the wheat from the light, inedible part of the head of wheat. In biblical times (and later), this was done by tossing the grain into the air. The wind carried the lighter, useless part away, leaving the heavier kernel. In both Matthew 3:12 and Luke 3:17, John the Baptist warns that God will eventually separate the wheat from the chaff (the good from the evil) and then burn the chaff.

Does John the Baptist have anything to do with the Baptist church?

The origin of the name is the connection. Both the Anabaptists (rebaptizers), from which the Baptists derive the name, and John the Baptist take their names from the Greek word *baptizo*, "to baptize, immerse, dip," and both John the Baptist and the Baptists baptize by immersion. The methodology is not the point, however. The Baptists do not believe in infant baptism, holding that one should understand and choose before being baptized.

How did John the Baptist die?

John the Baptist is a plain-speaking prophet. When Herod Antipas (son of Herod the Great) marries Herodias, his brother Philip's wife, John doesn't hesitate to speak out, reminding Herod that, by law, the marriage is forbidden.

Truly his father's son, Herod Junior has John seized and thrown into prison. However, not having quite the nerve of his father and being wary of the possible reaction among those who revere John as a prophet, he hesitates to have John killed. Herodias, who deeply resents John's accusations, is ticked but bides her time.

Herod's birthday arrives and Herodias lays on a little treat. She has her daughter, Herod's stepdaughter, dance at the birthday celebrations.

The girl must have put on quite the show, because the delighted Herod takes an oath to give her anything she desires. A dutiful daughter, she runs back to her mother for instructions. This is the moment Herodias has been waiting for. Without blinking an eye, one presumes, she tells her daughter to ask for the head of John the Baptist on a charger (platter).

Even Herod is a little stunned by this, but he can't go back on his oath — especially with everyone at the banquet watching. So he sends word to behead John who is still in prison, and the head is brought in on a platter and given to Herodias's daughter. She immediately hands it over to her mother, who was the one who wanted it in the first place.

How many days does Jesus spend in the desert before starting his ministry?

Jesus spends forty days fasting in the desert. This is no accident. Forty seems to be attached in the Bible to periods of testing, before a new beginning. It rained for forty days and forty nights when the Great Flood covered the earth. Noah waited forty days before opening a window in the Ark. Moses spent forty days and forty nights on the mountain with God. The Israelites spent forty years wandering in the desert before they entered the Promised Land. Jonah warned the people of Nineveh that they had forty days to repent — and they were reconciled with God. And Moses and Elijah, like Jesus, fasted for forty days before undertaking a great task.

Salome

Herodias's daughter has taken on a life of her own since the biblical account. I suppose that's to be expected when a nubile young dancing girl enters the scene.

She was never named in the Bible (though some ancient versions of Mark call her Herodias, like her mother). It was the Jewish historian Josephus who gave her name as Salome, though she was not called that regularly until the nineteenth century.

Neither was there anything approaching the "dance of the seven veils" in the Bible. Interestingly, there is a suggestion that this originated in a tale of the Assyrian goddess Ishtar, who was trying to visit her sister in the underworld. To get through the seven gates of the underworld, she was forced to drop a piece of clothing at every one, finally arriving in the underworld naked. How this story might have attached itself to the figure of Salome is a mystery.

It seems to be various traditions and cultures that transformed Salome into the epitome of seductiveness and placed her in the pantheon of femmes fatales.

Oscar Wilde, for instance, in his play *Salomé* (1896), portrays her as a schemer who lusts after John the Baptist and has him killed when he spurns her. Aubrey Beardsley's illustration for the play was fittingly decadent. Both the Wilde play and Richard Stauss's opera *Salome* (1905) make the most of the "dance of the seven veils."

Hollywood cast the archetypal vamp Theda Bara in the role of Salome in 1918, and the film image of Salome was set. In the 1953 film *Salome*, Rita Hayworth performs the dance as a striptease (though never removing her flesh-coloured dress), and in the 1961 film *King of Kings*, which was generally panned, Brigid Bazlen drew attention for her voluptuous Salome.

Something has truly become a cultural item when it appears as a reference in other works. In 1950's *Sunset Boulevard*, fading film star Norma Desmond is writing a screenplay of the Salome legend, and it is a scene from this that she performs after she goes mad. In 1974's disturbing *The Night Porter*, Charlotte Rampling dances for the guards at a concentration camp, wearing pieces of an SS uniform, and is rewarded with a severed head, a clear reference to the story of Salome.

The story of the actual Salome is a bit anticlimactic. Josephus records that, after her moment of dubious celebrity, she married twice (presumably the first husband died a natural death) and lived a long life.

What is the origin of the saying
"Get thee behind me, Satan"?

This is used to indicate that one is rejecting temptation. Although today the phrase is often used humorously, in reference to such things as cigarettes and chocolate cake, there was nothing humorous about its use in the Bible.

At the beginning of Jesus's ministry, he fasts in the desert for forty days. When Jesus emerges, the devil tempts him three times but Jesus stands firm. In Luke 4:8, Jesus says, "Get thee behind me, Satan: for it is written, Thou shalt worship the Lord thy God, and him only shalt thou serve."

Just before his crucifixion, he uses the same expression again. He has been preparing his disciples for his inevitable suffering and death in Jerusalem. When Peter protests that this shall not be, Jesus turns to him with the same command: "Get thee behind me, Satan" (Matthew 16:23; Mark 8:33). This seems a little harsh, but Peter is charged with not understanding the plans of God.

What are the three temptations
that Satan offers Jesus?

When Jesus comes out of the desert after fasting for forty days, he is no doubt ready for a snack, so Satan first challenges him to turn stones into bread. Then he takes Jesus up to the pinnacle of the Temple in Jerusalem and challenges him to leap off. If he is the son of God, Satan argues, God will protect him. Then he takes Jesus to a mountain and shows him the kingdoms that he could have if he consents to worship Satan. These temptations represent three major desires: goods and provisions, power, and wealth, but more than that they are all tests of God, which Jesus resists.

This shows that he is ready to start his ministry.

How old was Jesus when he began his teaching?

Luke 3:23 says, "And Jesus himself began to be about thirty years of age, being (as was supposed) the son of Joseph."

What was Jesus's first miracle,
and who asked him to perform it?

Early in his career, Jesus is at wedding in Cana in Galilee (John 2:1–11). It might well have been a family affair, because Jesus's mother is there too (though she is not referred to by name).

At some point they run out of wine at the wedding (oh no!), and Jesus's mother comes to Jesus and says, "They have no wine." Interestingly, there seems to be an unspoken message here, because Jesus answers, in effect, "Why are you asking me? It's not time yet."

Jesus's mother — let's call her Mary — persists, and says to the servants, "Do whatever he tells you." According to the Bible, of course, Mary has known all along who Jesus is and what he can do, but here she seems to be nudging him into revealing his gifts. And it works.

Jesus asks that six water pots be filled to the brim with water, and then tells the servants to draw from the pots. When they take the result to the governor of the feast (the person in charge, or host), it is wine of such quality that the governor of the feast calls in the bridegroom to complain. It was the custom to serve the best wine first, and then move on to the poorer. Presumably by then no one would be noticing the quality. He scolds the bridegroom for holding out on his guests.

There's something interesting about a mother pushing her son to supply alcohol.

Where do we get the expression
"Physician, heal thyself"?

This now is used to mean that one should mend one's own faults, rather than pointing out those of others. It seems to have been a Hebrew proverb.

In Luke 4:23, Jesus, who has returned to his hometown of Nazareth after his fame had begun to spread, says to those gathered around him in the synagogue: "Ye will surely say unto me this proverb, Physician heal thyself: whatsoever we have heard done in Capernaum, do also here in thy country." This is usually thought to mean that Jesus expects the crowd to ask him to prove himself. After all, they know him as the carpenter's son. This seems to be borne out when he then says, "No prophet is accepted in his own country." Oh, those hometown audiences.

What was the significance of Jesus choosing twelve followers for his inner circle?

The choice of the twelve apostles would have had a great deal of significance for the people. The twelve sons of Jacob, including Joseph, became the ancestors of the twelve tribes of Israel. By choosing twelve disciples, Jesus is showing that his teachings are for all Israel.

What is the difference between a disciple and an apostle?

Since the twelve are referred to as both disciples and apostles, this can be confusing.

Disciple means a student or learner, and applies to anyone who follows the message of a teacher. *Apostle* is taken from the Greek word *apostello*, "to send forth" or "to dispatch."

So, the twelve were disciples of Jesus. After Jesus returns to heaven, he delegates the task of spreading his message to the twelve, who then officially become apostles.

At the same time, any follower of Jesus, then or now, could be termed a disciple, and any of those in the early church who were "called" to spread the word could be termed apostles.

Bottom line: the twelve can be called both disciples and apostles. Though their special commission from Christ means that they have traditionally been called the Apostles, today the terms seem to be used interchangeably.

TOP 10 TREES MENTIONED IN THE BIBLE

1. **Olive trees:** Used mainly to produce olive oil. The oil was used for food and cooking, as the major source of fuel for oil lamps at night (the major source of lighting), and for religious ceremonies (anointing). At the end of The flood, when the dove returned to Noah's ark with the leaf of an olive tree, Noah knew that the waters were receding.
2. **Shittah tree (Acacia):** A very common tree in the desert. Used for cabinetry, it is also the tree the Lord commanded Moses to use to build devotional structures, including an altar and a tabernacle, and the Ark of the Covenant.
3. **Evergreen cypress:** a tree noted for its height, this is considered by some scholars to be the elusive source of the "gopherwood" that God commanded Noah to use in building the ark.
4. **Date palms:** An extremely important tree with a multitude of uses. The fruit is eaten as is, or can be made into cakes, spreads, paste, "honey" (date syrup), vinegar, or alcohol. Dried dates are also fed to livestock. The young date leaves can be cooked and eaten. The seeds can be ground and mixed with flour when wheat is scarce, or just used as animal feed. The fruit clusters (sans fruit) can be used as brooms. The leaves can be used to make mats, baskets, and roofing materials. Rope can also be made from this tree.
5. **Fig trees:** The tree's "fruit" (actually a flower of the fig tree, rather than a real fruit) is used as a food source and for traditional medicine. The trees produce two to three crops a year.
6. **Evergreen carob (or locust tree):** This is another important tree. The seed pods are used as food for humans and livestock, and were an important source of sugar. It is also known as St. John's Bread, as John the Baptist is believed by some traditions to have lived off them in the wilderness (they were referred to as "locusts," and the hopeful theory is that this is what John ate rather than hopping insects). Carob is also infamous as the usual replacement for chocolate in recipes. Also interesting: the term "carat," used for measuring the weight of diamonds, is derived from the ancient practice of using carob seeds as a standardized weight in transactions.
7. **Cedars:** Used for building. The famous Cedars of Lebanon grow to over 120 feet and were plentiful in biblical times, being widely used by the Phoenicians to construct ships and buildings (a cedar tree is shown on the Lebanese flag). The wood was also used by the Israelites in the construction of important temples and palaces.

8. **Almonds:** Almond trees are actually native to the Middle East, and are believed to be one of the very first cultivated fruit trees. For Israelites, the almond blossom was also a model for the construction of the temple menorah (see Exodus 25:31–35), the seven-branched candelabrum made of gold and used for the Tabernacle.

9 & 10. **These have been combined for a reason:** No mention of trees would be complete without the two most famous trees: **The Tree of Life**, and **The Tree of the Knowledge of Good and Evil**, that Genesis mentions were in the centre of the Garden of Eden.

What are the names of the twelve apostles?

This can sometimes be hard to pin down, since a few of the apostles, like Peter, have alternate names.

The twelve are: Peter, also known as Simon, Simon Peter, or Cephas; Andrew, who is Peter's brother; James and his brother John (the sons of Zebedee); Matthew, who is also Levi; Philip; Bartholomew, who is most likely the same person as Nathanael and possibly the brother of Philip; Thomas; James (sometimes called James the Less to distinguish him from James the brother of John); Thaddaeus (sometimes called Judas, but not to be confused with Judas Iscariot); and, finally, Judas Iscariot.

Apostle Spoons

Apostle spoons originated in Europe in the early fifteenth century. They are usually of silver, but sometimes of pewter, and the terminal of each spoon consists of the figure of an apostle holding his emblem (usually a symbol of his martyrdom). A full set includes thirteen spoons, bearing the figures of the twelve apostles and Jesus.

They were originally used as serving spoons, but by the sixteenth century they were being given as presents at the christening of godchildren. In fact, in Shakespeare's *Henry VIII*, when Cranmer balks at being made godfather of Princess Elizabeth because of the expense, the king teases him by saying, "Come, come my lord, you'd spare your spoons." This tradition faded by the end of the seventeenth century, but didn't die out completely. Apostle spoons are still around — and are considered very collectible.

Apostle spoons have become heirlooms in many families. In *The Tangled Web* by Lucy Maud Montgomery, "Aunt Becky," wishing to cause as much discord as possible, announces to whom she plans to leave her treasures. The apostle spoons are a coveted item.

How many of the Apostles were fishermen?

Because we don't know the occupations of some of the apostles, this question cannot be answered definitively. Certainly four of them were: Peter, Peter's brother Andrew; and the brothers James and John. It is thought some of the others were as well, but the Bible doesn't mention it.

Why has the fish become a symbol of Christianity?

Quickies
Did you know ...
• that, according to Colossians 4:14, Luke, the writer of the Gospel of Luke (and possibly Acts), was a physician?

Not only are at least a third of the Apostles fishermen, but when he called them to be his disciples, Jesus said, "Follow me, and I will make you fishers of men" (Matthew 4:19). Because of this, the fish was used as a symbol of early Christianity.

In addition, the Greek word for "fish," *ichthys*, can be read as an acrostic for "Jesus Christ, God's son, saviour" in Greek, and the symbol of a fish, represented by two intersecting arcs that overlap at one end to form a sort of tail, is now popularly known as the "Jesus fish" or the "sign of the fish."

This symbol has a fascinating history. Early Christians, who were persecuted by the Romans in the first few centuries after Christ, used the symbol to mark their meeting places and to indicate tombs of Christians. It can, in fact, be seen in the catacombs in Rome that date from the first century C.E. It was also used to determine if a person was friend or foe. When a Christian met a stranger, the Christian might draw one arc of the fish symbol on the ground. If the other person drew the other arc, they both knew they were safe. At a time when exposure as a Christian could mean a gruesome death, such a sign was invaluable.

Today, the symbol can be seen in such things as jewellery or bumper stickers and still is used to identify the wearer (or driver) as a Christian.

Which of the Apostles was a tax collector?

Matthew, also known as Levi, was a tax collector.

This was a particularly unpopular profession at the time, since tax gatherers or "publicans" (from the Latin *publicanus*) were Jews that collected taxes from their own people to hand over to the Roman rulers.

This can be seen in the Luke 5 when Jesus sees Mattew/Levi "sitting at the receipt of custom," and calls him to follow. After accepting the call, Levi throws a feast for Jesus in his own house to celebrate, "and there was a great company of publicans and of others that sat down with them." The position of tax collectors in the pecking order is clear when the Jewish leaders grumble and ask the disciples, "Why do ye eat and drink with publicans and sinners?"

What name does Jesus give to Peter?

In John 1:42, Jesus, having just called Simon Peter and Andrew to follow him, says to Simon Peter, "Thou art Simon the son of Jona: thou shalt be called Cephas, which is by interpretation, A stone." In Matthew 16:18, he says, "thou art Peter, and upon this rock I will build my church."

Because of this, Catholic tradition holds that Peter was, in fact, the first Pope.

Why is Peter pictured as the gatekeeper of Heaven?

We've all heard the jokes: "So, this man dies. And he goes up to the gate of Heaven and St. Peter says ..."

This taken from Matthew 16:19, in which Jesus says to Peter, "I will give unto thee the keys of the kingdom of heaven." Because of this, in paintings and sculptures, Peter is often portrayed holding keys.

What nickname does Jesus give the brothers James and John?

Jesus calls them "The Sons of Thunder." The Bible never says exactly why this is, but they seem to have been hot-headed. For instance, when Jesus is travelling to Jerusalem, he sends messengers ahead to a Samaritan town to find lodgings. The Samaritans have no love for Jerusalem, so they reject him. James and John immediately want Jesus to "command fire to come down from heaven, and consume them," and Jesus has to point out that he came to save lives, not take them. He must have heaved a sigh of frustration, but on the other hand, James and John were his loyal defenders.

What bird is named after Peter?

At one point in the gospels, the disciples are in a boat on the Sea of Galilee when they see Jesus walking towards them on the water. While the others watch, Peter jumps out of the boat and starts to walk towards Jesus.

Because of this he lends his name to the petrel, a seabird that flies low over the waves. Its dangling legs make it appear to be walking on the water.

Why do we talk about "hiding one's light under a bushel"?

Today this phrase is used to encourage to those who do not flaunt their gifts, and in fact do not do justice to their abilities through excessive modesty.

The phrase comes from Matthew 5:15. Jesus is preaching to his followers, and is indeed advising them not to hide their lights. However, he's not talking about abilities but about the message he is giving. As he continues in Verse 16, "Let your light so shine before men, that they may see your good works, and glorify your Father which is in heaven." In other words, a command that originally meant to reflect praise on God is now used to mean that one should not hide one's own gifts.

Where do we get the expression "Straight and narrow"?

This refers to the difficult path of virtue, as opposed to the wide and easy path of transgression. In Matthew 7:14, the phrase was actually "strait and narrow," since *strait* means narrow or tight (as in, a strait between two pieces of land or to be in "straitened circumstances"). As more subtle usage has fallen out of favour, the phrase has been changed to "straight and narrow." Either phrasing emphasizes the point that living a virtuous life is more difficult.

> **Quickies**
> *Did you know ...*
> • that the word *miracle* comes from the Latin *mirari*? This means "to wonder at."

Where did we get the expression "The blind leading the blind"?

This describes a situation in which those who know nothing are leading others who know nothing.

Jesus knew what happened when this occurred. In Matthew 15:14, referring to the Pharisees that had just criticized his teaching, he said to his disciples: "Let them alone: they be blind leaders of the blind. And if the blind lead the blind, both shall fall into the ditch." Sub-prime mortgages are a good example of this.

Which of the disciples had a "stage mother"?

It seems the sons of thunder, James and John, come by their personalities honestly. In Matthew 20:20–28, their mother approaches Jesus, accompanied by the boys. When Jesus asks what she wants, she says, "Grant that these my two sons may sit, the one on they right hand, and the other on the left, in thy kingdom." Needless to say, the other ten disciples are pretty ticked off at this naked jockeying for position.

Jesus heaves another sigh and explains that they've missed the point. The way to be great is to serve others.

The Jefferson Bible

In the late eighteenth century, Thomas Jefferson conceived of the idea of writing a review of the "Christian System," in which the "principles of pure deism" taught by Jesus would be stripped of anything to do with the supernatural. (It was, after all, the Age of Enlightenment, and Jefferson, raised as an Anglican, was influenced by the English deists.) In 1804 he composed a limited version of what he had in mind, which never satisfied him, and he resolved to try again.

To put together *The Life and Morals of Jesus of Nazareth* (the actual title of the work), he took a razor and physically cut and arranged the verses he selected from the books of Matthew, Mark, Luke, and John, putting them in chronological order and producing a straightforward narrative. Gone were the virgin birth, angels, prophecies, miracles, the Trinity, and anything about the divinity of Jesus. He called the actual moral teachings that remained "sublime."

Completed in 1820, the book was not published in Jefferson's lifetime, though he passed it around among his friends. His grandson inherited the work, and it was finally published by the National Museum in Washington in 1895.

It has become known as The Jefferson Bible, and is now available in paperback.

Where do we get the expression "Pearls before swine"?

Today this phrase refers to wasting things of quality on people that can't understand them. When it was used in the Bible (Matthew 7:6), it meant more particularly wasting the word of holy teachings on those who won't accept them. As Matthew 7:6 reads: "Give not that which is holy unto the dogs, neither cast ye your pearls before swine, lest they trample them under their feet, and turn again and rend you." A bit rough on the animals.

The famous writer Dorothy Parker, renowned for her sharp wit, is said to have employed this saying to good effect one evening when she met a female rival at the door to a nightclub. "Age before beauty," smirked the other woman, standing aside. "Pearls before swine," retorted Parker, sweeping into the club.

Why do we talk about a "wolf in sheep's clothing"?

This has become the classic description of someone who is not what he or she seems to be, who appears friendly or benign, but intends ill. Obviously, looking like a sheep is a very handy thing for a wolf, and he does not wish the sheep well. In Matthew 7:15, Jesus warns his followers against false prophets, "which come to you in sheep's clothing, but inwardly they are ravening wolves."

How many demons did Christ cast out of Mary Magdalene?

In Mark 8:2, Jesus is travelling around preaching with the twelve disciples, "and certain women, which had been healed of evil spirits and infirmities, Mary called Magdalene, out of whom went seven devils." This is considered of such importance that, when Mary Magdalene is the first to meet Jesus after his resurrection, it is mentioned again: "Now when Jesus was risen early the same day of the week, he appeared first to Mary Magdalene, out of whom he had cast seven devils" (Mark 16:9).

Where did the idea that Mary Magdalene and Jesus were married come from?

Thanks to Dan Brown and the *Da Vinci Code*, this idea has earned a great deal of prominence, but it is nowhere suggested in the gospels.

Brown, and others like him, are working from writings of the Gnostics, a sect that was declared heretical in 388 C.E. Only fragments of their writings remain, but several — *Pistis Sophia*, and the gospels of

Mary, Thomas, and Philip — speak of Mary Magdalene as an extremely important disciple who had a special relationship with Jesus. The Gospel of Philip does refer to her as Jesus' companion.

It is important to remember, however, that these writings are usually dated to the second and third centuries C.E.

Where do we get the expression "A whited sepulchre"?

This means a hypocrite. A whited sepulchre is a tomb that has been whitewashed to appear clean on the outside, but is full of bones and the dead. Jesus uses this phrase to describe those who profess to goodness and put on a show of sanctity, but are corrupt within.

Quickies
- In Joseph Conrad's *Heart of Darkness*, the narrator, Marlow, says "In a very few hours I arrived in a city that always makes me think of a whited sepulchre." This seems to be Brussels, and Marlow is suggested that it is beautiful but corrupt.

Quickies
Did you know ...
- that "Blessed are the peacemakers" was the personal motto of James I of England?

Quickies
Did you know ...
- that J. Paul Getty, named as the richest living American by *Fortune* magazine in 1957, is reported to have said, "The meek shall inherit the earth, but not the mineral rights"?

Why are the Beatitudes called the Beatitudes ?

The name is taken from the Latin *beatus*, meaning "blessed" or "happy." Not only does this reflect the beginning of each beatitude, "blessed [or happy] are ye ...," but the implication is that these are rules that will lead to a happy life.

Where do we get the expression "Salt of the earth"?

This is from Matthew 5:13, and is used to refer to a person or persons who are of essential value and trustworthiness.

Jesus, preaching to the multitudes, has just delivered the Beatitudes, listing all those who are blessed by God. He then says, "Ye are the salt of the earth." Some suggest that Jesus was referring to the great value of salt, but anyone who has eaten an unsalted dish doesn't need to look that far to understand the worth of salt, and how it gives flavour to everything. This interpretation is strengthened by the words that follow: "but if the salt has lost its savour, wherewith shall it be salted? It is thenceforth good for nothing, but to be cast out, and to be trodden under foot of men."

Where do we get the expression "A Good Samaritan"?

This refers to someone who does something to help another without any expectation of payment or other reward. We often see this expression in the newspapers, in reference to someone who saved a child from a burning building, or ran to the aid of a mugging victim. But as praiseworthy as these actions are, they lose something of the significance in the actions of the first Good Samaritan.

Jesus tells the story of the Good Samaritan (Luke 10:30–37) in answer to a lawyer (the defender of the formal code) who has been reminded that he should love God and his neighbour. He asks, "And who is my neighbour?"

Most of us know the plot of the story Jesus tells in response. A man travelling from Jerusalem to Jericho is attacked by thieves, who rob him and leave him battered by the side of the road. Both a priest and Levite (another type of priest), defenders of formal codes, pass by without helping him, but a Samaritan stops, tends him, and takes him to an inn, leaving money to pay for his care.

Jesus' audience would not have missed the significance of the rescuer being a Samaritan. The Samaritans were traditional enemies of the Jews, and Jews would often go to great lengths to avoid Samaritan territory. That the Samaritan rescues the Jew when even his own religious leaders did not shows that Jesus is broadening in a significant way the definition of who one should consider a "neighbour."

Where do we get the expression "Go the extra mile"?

This means to do more for someone than is required. In Jesus's day, when the land was under the control of Rome, by law, a Roman soldier could make anyone carry his equipment for one mile. Jesus, speaking in Matthew 5:41, tells his followers to go an extra mile, thus offering help beyond what was compelled. He wasn't speaking, of course, simply of Roman soldiers and laws, but of offering help to others freely.

What well-known hymn was inspired by the parable of the Prodigal Son?

In Jesus's parable of the Prodigal Son (Luke 15), one of the sons of a wealthy man, not wanting to wait until his father dies, commits the offence of asking for his inheritance in advance. When he receives it, he gallivants off to a foreign country and wastes everything on wild living.

Finally he is reduced to a pitiful condition, taking a job feeding pigs. A Jewish audience, to whom pigs are unclean, would see this as a sign that he had reached the lowest point possible.

Realizing that even his father's servants live better than he does, he decides to return home, beg forgiveness from his father, and ask for a job as a servant in his father's house. However, when his father sees him coming, he runs out to meet him, and not only forgives him but restores him to his previous place, and holds a feast to celebrate his return.

The brother of the prodigal is incensed, but the father assures him of his love and says the celebration is justified because "this thy brother was dead, and is alive again; and was lost, and is found," thus representing God, who accepts and forgives any repentant sinner.

These lines became the inspiration for the lyrics of the beloved hymn "Amazing Grace."

Amazing Grace

"Amazing Grace, that saved a wretch like me"

The lyrics to "Amazing Grace" were written by English clergyman John Newton around 1772.

When writing about a wretch who had fallen to extreme depths and then been saved by faith in God, Newton wrote from experience. *The Dictionary of American Hymnology* describes it as his autobiography in verse.

The London-born son of a shipping merchant who was often absent, Newton grew up a rebellious and profane young man. Eventually, his bad behaviour got him thrown into the Royal Navy. After deserting and undergoing punishment, he was traded to a slave ship and began a career in slave-trading. Even among this rough bunch, Newton earned the dubious distinction of being the most profane man the captain had ever encountered.

In 1748, his ship, *The Greyhound*, was caught in a violent storm and came close to sinking. Newton called on the mercy of God, and when the ship finally limped into port, Newton began to review his life and make some changes.

Though it took some time, with God's help and the love of a good woman — his wife, Polly — he managed to educate himself and to obtain a post as curate of the country parish of Olney, Buckinghamshire. There he was a great success as a preacher and began to write hymns (with a new resident of Olney, writer William Cowper) to be used at his services. These were collected and published in a volume entitled *Olney Hymns* in 1779. The hymns were immediately successful among the evangelical churches in Britain.

In America, the massive evangelical movement of the nineteenth century embraced "Amazing Grace." It had been sung to a variety of melodies, but in 1835, American William Walker set it to a tune known as "New Britain," and this is the melody we know today.

Interestingly, John Newton, former slave-trader, became an ardent proponent for the abolition of the slave trade and a supporter of William Wilberforce, who led the campaign to abolish the slave trade in Britain.

Though sung widely before then (the American Library of Commerce has three thousand versions, some recorded by folklorists Alan and John Lomax in 1932) the coming of radio and records helped the song cross over from religious to secular audiences. This crossover was so thorough that, although it was one of her most requested songs in the 1960s, singer Joan Baez didn't originally know it had once been a hymn. A 1947 recording by gospel singer Mahalia Jackson was widely played on the radio, spreading the popularity of the song along with Jackson's growing fame, and when Jackson used it during Civil Rights marches during the days of the American

Civil Rights Movement, it took on a political role. Folk singer Judy Collins recalls seeing civil-right activist Fannie Lou Hamer leading marchers in Mississippi in 1964 singing "Amazing Grace." Later it was used by protesters against the Vietnam War. It even turned up at Woodstock in 1969 during the performance of Arlo Guthrie. In subsequent years, it has been recorded by a wide variety of musicians, from Elvis Presley, Johnny Cash, Aretha Franklin, Willie Nelson, and Rod Stewart to the Royal Scots Dragoon Guards (on bagpipes).

Where do we get the expression "Practise what you preach"?

This is used to remind someone that they must act according to the standards they hold up to others. Towards the end of Jesus's ministry opposition to him starts to grow, especially from the Jewish religious leaders, the Pharisees, and the more powerful and priestly Sadducees. This was a rebuke that Jesus aimed directly at the Pharisees (Matthew 23:3). He saw them as hypocrites who kept the letter of the religious law publicly, but failed to behave according to its spirit.

Who anointed Jesus's feet with ointment?

Though many seem to take for granted that the repentant woman who anoints Jesus's feet at the Last Supper is Mary Magdalene, one of the followers of Jesus, the gospels say nothing of the kind — though they have varying stories.

In Matthew 26, Jesus is having supper at the home of Simon the Leper (cured, by the way) in Bethany, when "there came unto him a woman having an alabaster box of very precious ointment, and poured it on his head." The disciples are upset at the expense, saying that the money could be given to the poor, but Jesus says that they won't have him with them forever, and the woman is anointing him for burial.

In Luke 10:37, the woman is described only as "a woman in the city, which was a sinner." On learning that Jesus is at supper in the home of a local Pharisee, she brings an alabaster box of ointment, washes Jesus' feet with tears, dries them with her hair, and anoints them with the ointment. Naturally, the Pharisee gets all bent out of shape, because Jesus is letting a sinful woman touch him, but Jesus points out that someone whose sins are great will receive more forgiveness.

In John 11, Lazarus of Bethany is seriously ill, and his sisters Martha and Mary, send for Jesus, who is not in town at the time. Lazarus and his sisters are clearly dear friends of Jesus. In John 11:2, it says in an aside, "It was that Mary which anointed the Lord with ointment, and wiped his feet with her hair, whose brother Lazarus was sick." In the next chapter, Jesus is a guest at the home of Mary, Martha, and the risen Lazarus. Here John says quite clearly, "Then took Mary a pound of ointment of spikenard, very costly, and anointed the feet of Jesus, and wiped his feet with her hair." Now, Mary of Bethany is a respectable friend of Jesus's, far from a sinner of the town.

So who did the anointing?

Since the account in Luke says so clearly that the woman is a sinner, perhaps it is Mary Magdalene's purely traditional role as a sinner that fitted her for the part, although there is nothing in the Bible that says she was a sinner. The only thing in the Bible that suggests her connection with sin is the fact that Jesus cast seven devils out of her. Modern scholars connect the casting out of demons with the curing of illness, but this may be where her questionable reputation started.

In traditional art, Mary Magdalene is often pictured carrying a pot of ointment, but this is a reference to Jesus's burial rather than the anointing of Jesus's feet. It may be this that connected her to the sinful woman with the ointment in Matthew.

Quickies

Did you know …

- that we get the English word *maudlin*, from Mary Magdalene. Because of the tradition linking her to the weeping sinner who anointed Jesus's feet, Mary Magdalene was often portrayed in art as a weeping woman. Since Magdalene was once pronounced and sometimes spelled "Maudlin" in medieval English (and is still the way the name of Magdalen College in Oxford is pronounced), the association was made with weeping. In fairness to Mary Magdalene, she is not immediately associated with the modern usage that suggests "foolish sentimentality."

Mary Magdalene does, however, have the distinction of being the only person named who is a witness to Jesus's crucifixion, his burial, and the discovery of the empty tomb.

What is the significance of Jesus riding into Jerusalem on a donkey?

In the Old Testament, the prophet Zechariah predicts that the Messiah, or king, will enter Jerusalem "lowly and riding upon an ass, and upon a colt the foal of an ass" (Zechariah 9:9). This symbolizes someone who comes in peace, rather than riding on a warhorse.

Fans of Handel's *Messiah* will recognize the beginning of this verse, "Rejoice greatly, O daughter of Zion."

Why do the people wave palm branches when Jesus enters Jerusalem?

The palm branches are used as signs of victory and celebration. This triumphant entry takes place a week before the Crucifixion, and so the Sunday before Easter Sunday is still celebrated as Palm Sunday.

What is a "mite" in the story of the widow's mite?

In the story of the widow's mite, Jesus and his followers are in the Temple. Jesus wishes to emphasize that the poor woman's offering is extremely small compared to the offerings that are being poured into the coffers of the Temple by the more wealthy (and showy), but that her sacrifice is greater in proportion. The coin in the story was probably a *lepton*, which was the smallest coin at the time. (And, by the way, she gave two coins in the Bible.)

At the time that the King James Bible was being translated, there was, in fact, a coin called a *mijt*. It was known in the Netherlands, with which Britain traded regularly, and was the smallest of copper coins.

Interestingly, both the *lepton* and the *mijt* were made from metals that were not as valuable as silver. The lepton was made of bronze, and the mijt of copper. This adds another layer to the story. It was expected that one would give a silver coin at church, and the fact that the widow gave, in the translation, a *copper* coin, and a *mijt* at that, emphasizes her poverty.

Our word *mite*, meaning something small or modest, is taken from the name of the *mijt*.

Where do we get the expression "The left hand doesn't know what the right hand is doing"?

This has come to mean that one keeps the various areas or interests in one's life compartmentalized, and does not mix them. Negatively, it has come to refer to confusion, more specifically incompetent confusion, as in: "This project is a mess; the right hand doesn't know what the left hand is doing." What Jesus is originally talking about in Matthew 6:3 is the giving of alms. He is urging his followers not to be like the hypocrites, who give alms just to get praise, but to give without thinking of reward.

What event does Jesus predict?

As Jesus and the disciples stand near the Temple, Jesus says, "The days will come, in the which there shall not be left one stone upon another"(Luke 21:6) Although some interpret this as a prediction of the "final days" of the world, it is also seen as a prediction of the destruction of the Temple after the Jewish rebellion in 70 C.E., approximately forty years later.

Where do we get the expression "To take someone under your wing"?

This means to protect or mentor someone. This particularly maternal image comes from Matthew 23:37. Jesus has returned to Jerusalem at the end of his ministry. Knowing that he is about to be killed, he laments and says, "O Jerusalem, Jerusalem … how often would I have gathered thy children together, even as a hen gathereth her chickens under her wings, and ye would not!"

What occasion are Jesus and his disciples celebrating at the Last Supper?

Jesus enters Jerusalem on Passover week, and it is the Jewish celebration of the Passover — in which the Jews mark the time when the angel of God passed over the houses of the Israelites and killed the firstborn sons of the Egyptians — that they are observing in the upper room.

In Luke 22:11 Jesus send Peter and John to book a room. They are to go into the city, where they will see a man carrying a pitcher. They are to follow him to his home and then say, "The Master saith unto thee, Where is the guestchamber, where I shall eat the passover with my disciples?"

It all sounds very cloak-and-dagger, and opinion is divided as to whether Jesus foresaw this or had made previous arrangements.

Why is the number thirteen considered unlucky in some Christian traditions?

Blame Judas Iscariot, the disciple who was to betray Christ.

Tradition has it that Judas arrived late for the supper, and was thus the thirteenth to sit down at the table.

Other cultures also consider thirteen unlucky, the Ancient Persians and the Norse among them. In fact, fear of the number thirteen is so widespread that in *Abnormal Psychology*, published in 1910, the fear was given a name of its own: triskaidekaphobia.

Where do we get the term Eucharist?

When beginning the Last Supper, Jesus gave thanks over the bread and wine that he distributed to his disciples. The Greek word for "give thanks" is *eucharistesas*, so the ritual in which the meal is commemorated (or repeated) has become known in Catholic and Anglo-Catholic churches as the Eucharist.

What is Maundy Thursday?

This is one name for the holy day that falls on the Thursday before Easter Sunday and commemorates the Last Supper. This term is used mainly in England and in the Anglican and Catholic churches, though Holy Thursday is also used more familiarly.

At the Last Supper, Christ washes the feet of the disciples with his own hands. In a hot and dusty country, foot washing was important,

The Last Supper by **Leonardo da Vinci**

Painted by Da Vinci between 1495 and 1498 for his patron Duke Ludovico Sforza, *The Last Supper* is probably one of the most iconic works of art of the period.

The painting portrays the scene at the table when Jesus announces that one of the twelve will betray him. The reactions among the disciples ranges from surprise and shock to anger and faintness (John). Only Judas, fourth from the left, seems withdrawn, and his face is darkened. He clutches a small bag, which could represent his position as treasurer of the group or the money he was paid to betray Christ.

Rumours have swirled around the painting over the years. One of these claimed that the same model was used for Jesus and Judas. It makes a good story, but isn't true.

The rumour that is most prominent at the moment is that da Vinci embedded a code in the painting that hinted at a special relationship between Jesus and Mary Magdalene. The beardless figure sitting on Jesus' right, this theory holds, is not John as previously supposed, but Mary Magdalene.

The figure in question is admittedly androgynous, but a quick look at other works by da Vinci show that he had a particular fondness for portraying androgynous young men. It also neglects the fact that, if this figure is Mary Magdalene, the table is one disciple short.

Some even argue that the knife in Peter's hand is meant for Mary, since the Gnostic gospels portray them as having a troubled relationship. This ignores that the knife appears behind Judas's back and is also pointing toward Bartholomew, who died by flaying. These are both more likely interpretations, as is the possible allusion to Peter's impetuous attack on the high priest's servant, which is to come that very night. And yes, the chalice shown in front of Jesus is what became known as the Holy Grail.

The painting can be seen on the wall of the refectory of the church of Santa Maria delle Grazie in Milan.

but it was usually done by a servant. By washing the feet of the disciples, Jesus takes on that role, emphasizing that the life he represents is one of love and service.

Most scholars seem to agree that the name of Maundy Thursday derives from Jesus's words at the time: "A new commandment I give unto you, That ye love one another; as I have loved you" (John 13:34). In Latin, that phrase begins with "Mandatum vobis …"

Since the reign of Edward I in England, the monarch has distributed alms, known as the Royal Maundy or Maundy money, to deserving senior citizens on Maundy Thursday. (Interestingly, the recipients are one man and one woman for each year of the sovereign's age. Elizabeth II, as one of the longest-reigning monarchs, must be distributing quite a bit of Maundy by now.) Since 1822, especially minted Maundy money is given out, rather than ordinary currency — though the Maundy coins are legal tender.

Until the end of the reign of James I, the monarch would also wash selected deserving feet, in commemoration of Jesus's actions. The washing of feet is still a traditional part of the Maundy Thursday celebrations in many Christian churches

How much is Judas paid for betraying Christ?

The religious authorities pay Judas thirty pieces of silver. At the time, this would have been equivalent to about four months' wages.

What does the name *Gethsemane* mean?

After the Last Supper, Jesus and the disciples move outside the city wall to what is called the Mount of Olives, and specifically to the Garden of Gethsemane. The disciples are unaware of what is to happen, but of course Jesus isn't. Thus the word *Gethsemane* is sometimes used to refer to a time of trial in someone's life, as in, "That was his own personal Gethsemane."

What *Gethsemane* actually means is "oil press," after the oil production that gave the Mount of Olives its name.

Why do we say, "Many are called, but few are chosen"?

The modern meaning of this is: anyone can try something, but not everyone can succeed. However, the biblical source is a little more weighty. Jesus is telling a parable about the kingdom of heaven and who will be considered worthy (Matthew 22). In the parable, a king throws out a general invitation to the marriage of his son. One guest arrives without a wedding garment, showing he is unworthy, and is cast into everlasting darkness, "where there is weeping and gnashing of teeth" (that's a clue this is not just about a wedding). Matthew 22:14 then states: "For many are called, but few are chosen."

Where do we get the expression "The spirit is willing, but the flesh is weak"?

This refers to the difficulty of always living up to the high standards one has set for oneself and also to the physical difficulty of actually pulling off something to which we are committed. No matter how much we mean well, sometimes, being human, we fail or simply fail in strength.

This is taken from Matthew 26:41. Jesus has gone into the Garden of Gethsemane to pray, knowing that he will soon be betrayed and will die. He asks his disciples to stay and watch with him, but they fall asleep. On finding them, he says to Peter, "Watch and pray, that ye enter not into temptation: the spirit indeed is willing, but the flesh is weak."

Is it possible to sweat blood?

As he prays in the Garden of Gethsemane, preparing for what is to come, Jesus is suffering a great deal. Luke 22:44 reads, "And being in agony he prayed more earnestly: and his sweat was as it were great drops of blood falling down to the ground."

The wording suggests strongly that this is not a literal description.

It is interesting, however, that there is a very rare condition called *hematidrosis*, in which a person under extreme stress can indeed sweat blood. One such case is recorded by Leonardo da Vinci, who had scientific interests. He described a soldier who sweated blood before going into battle.

What act of violence does Peter perform when the soldiers come to arrest Christ?

When the religious leaders and the temple guards come to Gethsemane to seize Christ, Peter takes a sword and cuts off the ear of the high priest's servant.

Jesus stops any further violence by saying to Peter, "Put up thy sword into his place: for all they that take the sword shall perish with the sword" (Matthew 26:52). This, of course, is where we get the expression "Those who live by the sword, die by the sword."

In the gospel of Luke, Jesus touches the servant's ear and heals it.

Where do we get the expression "Turn the other cheek"?

This well-known phrase comes from Jesus's command (Luke 6:29) that his followers not retaliate against violence, and, by extension, any act of aggression. This is a key verse in support of pacifism, along with "Thou shalt not kill."

Who was the first "streaker"?

There was an anonymous young man following Jesus who had "a linen cloth cast about his naked body." When the guards seized him, he left the linen cloth behind, and "fled from them naked" (Mark 14:51–52). Mischievous scholars have suggested that, because this detail does not appear in any of the other gospels, it is Mark himself who "fled naked." Of course, this will never be proven.

Where do we get the expression "To wash one's hands of something"?

This means to absolve oneself of responsibility or disassociate oneself from something.

Because Israel is under Roman rule, the Romans appoint a governor to carry out their business. In Jesus's day, the governor is a man named Pontius Pilate.

Quickies
Did you know ...
• that in the gospel of Luke, Herod Antipas (son of Herod the Great) is involved in the sentencing of Jesus. He, of course, is the same man who was responsible for the death of John the Baptist, Jesus' kinsman.

When Jesus is brought before him to be sentenced, Pilate is in a tight spot. The religious leaders and people (influenced by the priests) clearly want to have Jesus condemned. However, Pilate is not at all sure there is a case against Jesus, and, perhaps more importantly, his wife has just sent him a message saying: "Have nothing to do with that just man: for I have suffered many things this day in a dream because of him."

What to do, what to do? First, since it is a custom for the governor to release a prisoner at Passover, he offers to release Jesus. The people, however, ask instead for a notorious prisoner named Barabas.

Pilate passes the buck, as have so many past and present. Calling for a basin of water, he publicly washes his hands, declaring himself innocent "of the blood of this just person" (Matthew 27:24) and hands Jesus over to be crucified.

Where do we get the expression "Give up the ghost"?

In the Bible, and traditionally, this means to die. The phrase is not uncommon in the Bible, but perhaps its most striking use is at the moment of Jesus's death on the cross. Matthew 27:50 says, "Jesus, when he had cried again with a loud voice, yielded up the ghost." Mark 15:37 reads, "And Jesus cried with a loud voice, and gave up the ghost."

Quickies
• The two names used for the place where Jesus is crucified — Golgotha and Calvary — both mean "skull" in Aramaic and Latin respectively.

In the nineteenth century, the expression attached itself to inanimate objects, so that today one can speak humorously of a toaster "giving up the ghost."

Where does the name Easter come from, and why the bunnies and eggs?

This is another case, like Saturnalia, where the early church borrowed from their pagan neighbours.

To celebrate the resurrection of Jesus from the dead, the Christian missionaries to Britain piggy-backed on an Anglo-Saxon celebration and borrowed its name. Eostre was an Anglo-Saxon fertility goddess, whose religious festival was held on the vernal equinox, when the world was bursting with new life. This suited the early Christians, because not only was the celebration of Jesus' resurrection held on the first day of the week following the beginning of Passover, but the symbolism of new life made for a perfect fit.

In contrast, the Romance languages borrowed from the Hebrew word for Passover, *Pesach*. This can be seen in the French word for Easter, *Pâques*.

This also explains the prevalence of eggs and bunnies at Easter. Both were symbols of fertility. Eggs symbolize new life (and colouring them represents the bright colours of spring), while rabbits are noted for their enthusiastic propagation.

TOP 10 "BAD" WOMEN OF THE BIBLE

1. **Eve:** The first "bad girl." As the Bible reports it, Adam and Eve were happy enjoying everything in abundance. Then Eve, with help from the serpent, has a weak moment and ignores God's instructions not to eat the fruit of the Tree of the Knowledge of Good and Evil. Whoops! The story illustrates that to all actions there are consequences, some of which are very long term indeed.
2. **Delilah:** Ah, Delilah, a biblical "black widow." She was hired by the Philistines (her own people, by the way) to learn the secret of Samson's almost supernatural strength. She captured Samson's heart, and by learning about his hair, caused his demise. Was this the original "bad hair day"?
3. **Herodias:** A Jewish Roman citizen, she had a fondness for uncles, specifically, marrying them. Both her husbands (Herod Philip and Herod Antipas) were her uncles. As we have seen, when John the Baptist denounced her marriage to Herod Antipas as unlawful, she used her daughter to get John beheaded.
4. **Salome:** Daughter of the aforementioned Herodias, Salome was

instrumental in the plot to have John the Baptist put to death.

5. **Bathsheba:** As the story goes, King David became enamoured with Bathsheba, who was married to Uriah, a Hittite. David then had an affair with Bathsheba, who became pregnant with his child while Uriah was at war, fighting for Israel. After trying to hide the misdeed with a clever ruse (which failed due to Uriah's honourable behaviour), David arranged for Uriah to die in battle. Not one of David's finest actions as king. To be fair, the Bible doesn't record what Bathsheba thought about it all. You didn't say "No" to a king.

6. **Potiphar's Wife:** The main player in a charming story of unrequited lust and false witness. Potiphar's wife (who is never actually named in the Bible) tried to seduce Joseph. When Joseph refused, she accused him of trying to rape her, and Joseph was imprisoned. Fate intervened, and Joseph's actions in prison (his skill at interpreting the meaning of dreams) impressed Pharaoh. This resulted in a complete turnaround in Joseph's fortunes, when Pharoah made him viceroy of Egypt.

7. **Lot's Wife:** Why salt? We all know that Lot's wife was the sole person of the Lot family who defied God's instructions not to turn back and look upon Sodom and Gomorrah and their destruction, and thus she became the favourite seasoning of the middle ages. Her wickedness seems fairly mild by today's standards, yet the Old Testament Bible judges disobedience very harshly.

8. **Lot's Daughters:** After Lot's wife is changed into a pillar of salt, his two virgin daughters, afraid that their family will have no descendants, decide that the best way to ensure children is to get their father drunk and have him sire their offspring (their fiancés were killed in Sodom and Gomorrah). Two boys were born, Moab and Ammon, and these two founded nations of the Moabites and the Ammonites. Still, your wife turns into a pillar of salt and your daughters seduce you?! It would be hard to explain this to your co-workers. "Oh, yeah, and did I tell you …"

9. **Jezebel:** A Phoenician princess, the daughter of a Sidonian king, she married Ahab, who became king of Israel. As we have seen, Jezebel worshipped a number of gods, including her favourite, Baal, at a time when the worship of foreign gods was struggling with the worship of Yahweh to gain control of the hearts of the Israelites. After proving herself to be a ruthless and capable leader, she was finally murdered in a palace coup led by Jehu by being thrown from a high balcony.

10 **Gomer:** This "wicked woman" was a prostitute who married the prophet Hosea. Sometime later she had an adulterous relationship. Hosea then divorced Gomer, but in the end had a change of heart, forgave her, and took her back. Everyone likes happy endings! (By the way, it is believed this whole story is an allegory about God and Israel, represented by Hosea and Gomer respectively.)

Why is it significant that Jesus appears first to a woman, Mary Magdalene?

In Jewish and Roman law, the testimony of a woman had less value.

Some interpreters argue that the fact Jesus appeared first to a woman carries more weight, since anyone trying to falsify a case for the resurrection would have arranged to have the testimony of a man.

Why is the disciple Thomas referred to as Doubting Thomas?

In John 20, the disciples (except Thomas, it seems) are all gathered together, hiding from the people who sought Jesus's death. The doors are closed, but suddenly Jesus is standing among them. His first words are "Peace be unto you." Then he shows them his hands and his side, which bear the marks of the crucifixion. The disciples rejoice to see Jesus (John 20:20).

Along comes Thomas, and the others tell him what they have seen, but Thomas is not convinced. As he says, "Except I shall see in his hands the print of the nails, and put my finger into the print of the nails, and thrust my hand into his side, I will not believe."

Okay. Eight days later, the disciples are again shut in a room, but this time Thomas is with them. Again, Jesus appears in the room and he invites Thomas to put his finger into the nail holes in his hands and to put his hand into the wound in his side.

Finally, Thomas, the original "show-me" man, is convinced. But the label sticks.

How long does Jesus remain on earth after his resurrection?

Jesus remains on earth for forty days after his resurrection. This, of course, is the same length of time that he spent in the wilderness before beginning his ministry. As mentioned earlier, in the Bible the number forty seems to signal some major shift or new beginning.

the early church: acts, Romans, letters to the churches, Revelation

Where did Christ ascend to Heaven?

Christ stays on earth forty days after the Crucifixion, continuing to teach his followers. Then he ascends to Heaven, after giving the disciples what in the church is called "the Great Commission" — to spread the gospel "unto the uttermost part of the earth."

Luke says this took place in the vicinity of Bethany. Acts 1:12 says it took place on Mount Olivet (or Mount of Olives), about a "Sabbath day's journey" from Jerusalem. They're both right. Bethany and Mount Olivet could be considered in the same area.

Who replaced Judas Iscariot as the twelfth apostle?

At the Ascension, Jesus basically says to his followers, "Go back to Jerusalem and wait for a sign." As they stand around gaping afterwards (and who wouldn't), two mysterious men appear and say, to paraphrase, "What are you waiting for? He'll be back." So the disciples, now officially apostles, return to Jerusalem.

It's while the eleven remaining disciples are gathered in an upper room in Jerusalem with "the women," Mary the mother of Jesus, his "brethren" (and, according to Acts, about 120 others) that Peter points out that they're one man short. They choose two, and cast lots, and Matthias is appointed to take the place of Judas.

What is considered the birthday of the Christian church?

The sign that Jesus said would come to his followers was the Holy Ghost, which would give them the power to carry out the Great Commission.

At Pentecost or Shavuot, which is a Jewish holiday marking the gathering of the early crops of wheat and barley (also known as the Feast of the First Fruits), the disciples are again all gathered together. Suddenly there is the sound of a rushing wind, a flame appears on the head of each person, and they begin "to speak with other tongues, as the spirit gave them utterance" (Acts 2:4). It is, of course, the promised Holy Ghost that has come. (A flame appearing on the head of a person was a sign of divine blessing to the Romans.)

Because of the holiday, Jerusalem is packed with travellers from all over the Roman world, which was pretty big at the time. They are amazed to hear the disciples speaking in languages they can understand. Some of them even think the disciples are drunk, though Peter protests that "it is but the third hour of the day." As well as being a sign of the Holy Spirit, this gift of tongues foreshadows the fact that the apostles will eventually spread out into the known world.

After Peter speaks to the multitude that is gathered, those that believe are baptized, and the Bible says that three thousand "were added unto them." The rest is history.

This is why Pentecost is considered the birthday of the Christian Church.

> **Quickies**
> *Did you know ...*
> • that the quote "your young men shall see visions, and your old men shall dream dreams," was part of Peter's address to the crowd at Pentecost (Acts 2:17). It was quoted in speeches by John F. and Robert Kennedy, and was used at the funeral of John F. Kennedy in 1963.

What does *Pentecost* mean?

Pentecost is the Greek name for the Jewish holiday of Shavuot, which falls fifty days after Passover. The word *Pentecost* in Greek means "fifty."

Who is Gamaliel?

After Pentecost, Peter and John particularly go around preaching about Christ. The two of them even heal a man who has been lame for forty years and has sat at the entrance to the temple begging alms for most of that time. Everyone in Jerusalem knows who he is. The religious authorities have them arrested, but the lame man is standing right there, saying "Yes, they healed me."

They are released under stern warnings not to preach any more, but they persist, so the religious authorities have the apostles thrown in prison. Nice try. In the night, the "angel of the Lord" releases them, and the next day there they are preaching in the temple again. The religious authorities are fed up, and they start to plot how to kill them.

At that point a voice of great reason is heard.

Gamaliel is one of the most respected rabbis of the time. In Acts, he is introduced as "a Pharisee, named Gamaliel, a doctor of the law." At this juncture, Gamaliel says basically, "Leave them alone. If what's they're doing in is human in origin, then it will fail, but if it comes from God, nothing you can do will stop it."

Jewish tradition would later say, "When Gamaliel died, so did the glory of the Law."

Who is the first Christian martyr?

As their numbers grow, the disciples are having trouble seeing to the care and feeding of all their followers. As they say, "It is not reason that we should leave the word of God and serve tables" (Acts 6:2). So they decide to appoint seven administrators to look after the day-to-day practicalities, while they devote themselves to "prayer and to the ministry of the word." One of the seven chosen is Stephen, "a man full of faith."

Unfortunately, while preaching that Jesus is the Messiah, Stephen offends an influential group, who takes him before the religious authorities and charges him with blasphemy. This group also stacks the deck by bribing witnesses to speak out against Stephen.

When he is given a chance to defend himself, Stephen not only fails to recant, but tells the authorities that they're just like all the others through history who have rejected God.

That does it. They drag Stephen outside the city walls (plugging their ears so they can't hear his blasphemy) and stone him to death.

What future church leader witnesses the death of the first martyr?

Stoning a man to death is hot work, and those who are stoning Stephen take off some of their clothes and lay them at the feet of a young man named Saul, who is watching the proceedings. This is not just a case of "Hey, kid. Hold my coat." To lay a garment at the feet of another is a sign of respect that suggests Saul is in charge of the execution.

When a wave of persecution of the Christians races through Jerusalem, Saul is front and centre, dragging people out of their homes and off to prison.

Given the enthusiasm he shows in persecuting Christians (he is said to have "made havock of the church"), it is the more surprising that Saul becomes Paul, one of the most influential Christians of the first century.

Why do we speak of a "Damascus experience"?

Eager to persecute Christians, Saul starts out for the city of Damascus. He is carrying letters from the high priest to the synagogues there, authorizing him to arrest any Christians and carry them in chains to Jerusalem.

As he gets close to Damascus, he is blinded (literally) by a brilliant light from heaven, and a voice asking, "Saul, Saul, why persecutest thou me?" When Saul asks who is speaking, the voice answers, "I am Jesus whom thou persecutest." When the light disappears, Saul's companions lead him into the city, where God sends a man named Ananias to heal him of his blindness.

Saul is baptized and, from this point, he becomes as zealous a Christian as he was a persecutor of Christians.

The expression "a Damacus experience" or a "Damascus road experience" is used to describe a life-changing event or realization, one that totally changes a person's life from the course it was on.

This dramatic scene has been portrayed by many artists, but perhaps the most striking is the depiction by Caravaggio.

When did Saul become Paul?

He always was Paul. Paul is the Roman form of the Semitic name *Saul*, and Saul was both Jewish and a Roman citizen. Acts calls him Saul until he sails to Cyprus and meets a Gentile convert. After that point he is called Paul.

When was the name *Christian* first used?

The followers of Christ are first called Christians in Antioch (Acts 11:26). Before that, the church is known only as "the Way."

Who was the first of the twelve apostles to be martyred?

In Acts 12, there is a persecution of the church by Herod. It was Herod Agrippa I, grandson of Herod the Great, who ordered the Massacre of the Innocents, and son of Herod Antipas, who had John the Baptist put to death and mocked Jesus. These guys had a bad record.

He has the apostle James, the brother of John, killed by the sword, and seeing that this was a popular move with the crowd, he arrested Peter too. Peter escapes, thanks to divine intervention, and this is the last time he appears in Acts.

James was therefore the first of the twelve apostles to die (not counting Judas).

Where do we get the expression "The powers that be"?

This refers to whatever authority that is in power.

In his letter to the church in Rome, Paul writes: "Let every soul be subject unto the higher powers. For there is no power but of God; the powers that be are ordained of God" (Romans 13:1). Remember, the early church was walking a very fine line. Although its primary allegiance was to God, the last thing it wanted was to get a reputation as a sect that wished to cause civil disobedience. The later experiences of the Roman Christians with the lions showed what happened when the "powers that be" decided to persecute the church.

What Happened to the Twelve Apostles?

Being a disciple of the new church was not always a healthy thing to be in the first century. Of the twelve apostles, tradition says that only one, John, died of natural causes (though there is debate about Matthew).

Only one of these deaths is actually recorded in the New Testament, that of James. The traditions that surround them are taken from other sources (e.g., Origen, Tertullian, Clement of Rome).

Peter/Simon Peter

Peter disappears in Acts, but the tradition is that he and Paul travelled to Rome and founded the church there. It is almost certain that he died there in 64 C.E., being martyred under the Emperor Nero, but the other details are not as firm. The Great Fire of Rome occurred that year, and it is likely that the Christians were blamed, as usual.

He is said to have been crucified upside down, because he did not consider himself worthy to die in the same way as Christ.

James, son of Zebedee

As we have seen, James was the first apostle to die, under Herod Agrippa I. The Bible says he dies by the sword, but this more specifically means beheading.

The biblical record of his death in 44 C.E. hasn't stopped a belief spreading that he travelled to Spain, becoming a hero there, and in fact is buried at Santiago de Compostela. Since his symbol is a scallop shell, pilgrims to his shrine at Compostela wore, and still wear, a scallop shell.

John, son of Zebedee

Tradition says that John was the youngest of the Apostles, the last to die, and the only one to die of natural causes. He spent much of his later years in Western Asia Minor (what is today Turkey), apart from some years in prison on the island of Patmos. He is thought to have lived to the age of 94, and died of old age at Ephesus around 100 C.E.

Andrew

Andrew is said to have preached through Asia Minor and Scythia and along the Black Sea. He is also supposed to have founded the church at Constantinople.

According to tradition, he was crucified in Greece on an X-shaped cross, which has become known as the St. Andrew's Cross. Since he is the patron saint of Scotland, (among other places), the St. Andrew's Cross became the national flag of Scotland and was incorporated into the Union Jack, representing Scotland.

Philip

Philip is said to have gone to preach in Greece and Syria. There are two stories about his death, both traditional. One is that he was crucified upside down, and one is that he was beheaded. Both accounts place the scene of his death in Hierapolos in Southwestern Turkey.

Bartholomew (Nathaniel)

Bartholomew supposedly went on a missionary tour to India and brought Christianity to Armenia. He was supposedly martyred in Albanopolis in Armenia. One account has him beheaded, but a popular tradition has him flayed alive and crucified upside down.

Matthew

Later in his life, Matthew is said to have preached in Ethiopia south of the Caspian Sea (not the one in Africa), Macedonia, and Persia. There is disagreement on the manner of his death. Some traditions say he was martyred, though on different dates.

Thomas

There is a long-standing tradition that Thomas pushed his mission as far as India, and was killed with a spear at Mylapore.

James the Lesser

The most credible traditions about James are that he served as bishop of the church at Jerusalem and was martyred there.

Jude

Tradition suggests that he visited Beirut and Edessa, and may have been martyred in Persia.

Simon (the Zealot)

Early writings seem to have him preaching widely throughout the known world, but none of the reports can be confirmed. Most agree he was martyred, some say in 74 C.E. Tradition says he was crucified and then sawn into pieces.

Judas Iscariot

Judas, of course, hanged himself after he betrayed Jesus.

What do we mean by "As you sow, so shall you reap"?

Taken from Galatians 6:7, this is the Bible's version of "What goes around, comes around."

Where do we get the expression "All things to all men"?

This phrase is a bit slippery. In I Corinthians 9:22, Paul uses it to describe how he has made himself accessible to all those to whom he preaches, so that he might reach some. It could, therefore, be taken to mean something positive.

However, there is a negative side to this phrase. It has come to mean someone who can't be trusted, since they try to please everyone. Perhaps this relates to Jesus' words in Luke 6:26: "Woe unto you when all men shall speak well of you!"

Where did the idea of celibacy for priests begin?

In one of his letters to the church at Corinth, Paul recommends celibacy for those doing the work of God, so that they can focus on their service. He also acknowledges that this is difficult for some and that others like Peter can combine service and marriage with no problem.

Over the centuries that followed, many took this advice seriously, but it wasn't until the eleventh century that Pope Gregory VII made celibacy a requirement for the clergy.

Interestingly, the Protestant Reformation lost no time in doing away with this rule. There might be some explanation for this in the fact that Martin Luther, who had been a monk, married a former nun. He had to help her escape from her convent through a window.

The other line of Paul's that is also quoted is, "It is better to marry than to burn." This isn't exactly a ringing endorsement of marriage, but Paul was writing to the Christians in a notably licentious city. Marriage is seen as a protection against the sexual temptations that lay all around them. (In fact, in I Timothy 4:3, Paul seems to be warning Timothy against people who forbid marriage.)

Where do we get the expression "A thorn in the flesh"?

This refers to a problem or annoyance that causes irritation and won't go away (and yes, that person in the next office counts). In I Corinthians 12:7, the original thorn in the flesh is described as the messenger of Satan, sent to keep us humble and aware of our failings. Does the person in the next office seem less annoying now?

Quickies

Did you know ...

• that the city of Corinth, to which Paul wrote in I and II Corinthians, was so well known for prostitution that the Greeks referred to sexual relations as "to corinthianize."

Where do we get the word *bishop*?

In I Timothy 3, Paul lays out two levels of leadership in the church. The top level of overseers is related to the Greek word *episkopos*, and it is from this that we get the words *bishop* and *Episcopal*.

Where do we get the expression "The love of money is the root of all evil"?

The meaning of this saying is clear, but interestingly, it is often misquoted. If you thought it was "Money is the root of all evil," you are not alone. In I Timothy 6:10, Paul is writing to Timothy offering advice on what to watch for in the fledgling Christian community in Ephesus. His emphasis here is on the traps that money can create, and the place it takes in people's lives, rather than on money itself.

Where do we get the expression "Fight the good fight"?

Although addressed by Paul to Timothy (I Timothy 6:12), urging him to be strong in his work with the new church at Ephesus, and adopted by evangelical groups to refer to their work spreading the gospel, this phrase is also used in a more general way. It is often employed by groups striving for justice or for the triumph of a particular political outlook. More generally still, life being what it is, it is used to encourage those undergoing a particularly rough period or trying experience.

Considering Paul was sitting in prison awaiting execution under the Emperor Nero at the time he wrote these words, they are even more impressive.

What are the Four Horsemen of the Apocalypse?

The book of Revelation was written by the apostle John while he was in prison on the island of Patmos. It is a highly symbolic work (John says that he is recounting a dream) and purports to represent the events leading up to the end of the world.

Quickies

Did you know ...

- that the James who wrote the Epistle of James in the New Testament was the brother of Jesus and the leader of the church in Jerusalem. The writer of Jude identifies himself as a brother of this James, which suggests he was also Jesus's brother.

One of the enduring images, and one that has been used through the centuries to denote destruction, is that of the Four Horse men of the Apocalypse (Revelation 6).

The first horseman is riding a white horse and carrying a bow. He receives a crown and sets out conquering. He symbolizes war.

The second horseman is riding a red horse. He is given a giant sword and goes out to remove peace from the world and set people violently against each other. He symbolizes bloodshed and violence.

The third horseman is riding a black horse and carries a weighing scale. Because the verse that follows refers to the high price of wheat and barley, he is seen to symbolize famine.

The fourth horseman is riding on a pale horse and labelled Death. Hell comes with him. He is given power over one-quarter of the world, to kill by any method possible.

The dramatic nature of Revelation has made it a popular subject for artists down through the centuries. One of the most famous renderings of the Four Horsemen of the Apocalypse is a woodcut done by German artist Albrecht Dürer around 1497–98. It is the third woodcut from a series entitled, fittingly enough, *The Apocalypse*.

TOP 10 MISCONCEPTIONS ABOUT THE BIBLE

(For more details, check the text.)

1. Christmas is the day Jesus was born.
2. The forbidden fruit was an apple.
3. The Red Sea parted, à la Cecile B. DeMille's 1956 epic film, *The Ten Commandments*, with massive walls of water mysteriously held back for Moses and his people to pass.
4. There were three wise men ... and they were kings ... from the Orient.
5. Jesus was born in a stable.
6. The wise men were present at the birth of Jesus.
7. Noah's Ark had two of every animal.
8. There are Ten Commandments. Ten really does sound like a good, round number, but there are really twelve separate rules to follow. Tradition groups them into ten (given in the text). See Exodus 20:1–17 and Deuteronomy 5:1–22.
9. Mary Magdalene was a repentant prostitute
10. "Money is the root of all evil."

What city is symbolized by the Great Whore?

John describes the Great Whore as riding on a scarlet seven-headed beast with seven horns (Revelation 17), and then says in Revelation 17:9, in case the reader didn't get it, "The seven heads are seven mountains on which the woman sitteth."

Early readers would no doubt immediately made the connection with Rome.

In the ancient world, Rome was often referred to as "the city set on seven hills," because of the seven hills within the city walls (legend says that Romulus founded Rome on one of these hills, the Palatine).

What is the Mark of the Beast?

John describes a great Beast of the Earth, who will one day make everyone bear his mark on their right hand or forehead if they want to receive the necessities of life. This mark is specified as the number 666.

Much debate has swirled over the identification of the Beast. To those who see Revelation as a prophecy, this identifies the great Evil One who will arise in the end times. Unfortunately, this gives many people a stick to beat anyone they don't like. Most important figures (or things) in world affairs have been identified with the Beast at some point, from Martin Luther to the World Wide Web.

Others believe John was indicating Nero, who was happily persecuting Christians at the time (including John). Support for this comes from numerology. When the letters of Nero's name in Aramaic are assigned numerical values, they add up to 666.

Somewhere between these two beliefs is the view that John was indicating Nero, but using him as a stand-in for any persecutor of the church, past, present, or future.

"The Battle Hymn of the Republic"

In 1861, Julia Ward Howe visited a Union Army camp and heard the soldiers singing the well-known song "John Brown's Body" as an unofficial anthem. With her at the review was Rev. James Freeman Clarke, who suggested she write more uplifting words for the soldiers to sing.

During the night of November 18, 1861, she awoke with the words of the song in her mind, and leapt out of bed in near-darkness to write them down. The words of the first verse, "Mine eyes have seen the glory of the coming of the Lord. / He is trampling out the vintage where the grapes of wrath are stored," draw on Revelation 14:14–20.

The song was first published on the front page of the *Atlantic Monthly* in February 1862.

the Bible and culture

Note that as mentioned frequently, until the twentieth century, the influence of the Bible was so all-pervasive that a knowledge of the Bible and biblical allusions was taken for granted. We'll have to be selective.

How did Shakespeare use the Bible?

Shakespeare lived at a time when any educated person had learned and absorbed the Bible. And Shakespeare was educated. Despite the efforts by some to portray him as a rough-and-ready rural bumpkin and playhouse rat, whose natural genius lifted him above his circumstances, Shakespeare came

> **Quickies**
> *Did you know ...*
> • that French writer Victor Hugo (1802–1990) said, "England has two books, the Bible and Shakespeare. England made Shakespeare, but the Bible made England."

from a respectable — and even prominent — Stratford family, and received a solid education in the village grammar school. He would have been thoroughly grounded in both the Bible and Classical literature, to the point that they became a part of him and a constant source of examples, references, and language. His use of the Bible is organic. He doesn't so much quote the Bible as strike off it in his own way, knowing his audience would know the reference. Shakespeare was far too great an artist to lard his work with clunky quotes.

Because of this, it is difficult to point to Biblical allusions in his work, not because they aren't there, but because they are too plentiful, as are references to the Anglican *Book of Common Prayer*. Remember too, as a modern reader, that the Bible he used the most was not the King James Bible, which was not issued until five years before his death in 1616, but the Geneva (or Great) Bible, which was the official Bible of the Church of England under Henry VIII.

Some examples of Shakespeare using the Bible:

- *As You Like It* (Act 2: Scene 1) reads: "Here feel we but the penalty of Adam, / the Season's difference, as the icy fang /

And churlish chiding of the winter wind." The allusion to the Fall in Genesis is clear.

- In Act 3: Scene 3 of *Hamlet*, the guilt-wracked Claudius says: "O, my offence is rank, it smells to heaven; / It hath the primal eldest curse upon't, / A brother's murther."

- *Measure for Measure* is the only one of Shakespeare's plays that comes from the Bible, and even then, it isn't a direct quote. It is drawn from Matthew 7:2 "For with what judgment ye judge, ye shall be judged; and with what measure ye mete, it shall be measured to you again."

Quickies

Did you know ...

- that it has been suggested that Shakespeare was one of the translators of the King James Bible. This is probably because of a coincidence that was first pointed out in 1900 in the *Publisher's Circular*. Someone with too much time on their hands noticed that, in Psalms 46, the forty-sixth word from the beginning is "shake" and the forty-sixth word from the end is "spear." Because the two words were placed in different positions in previous translations, it was suggested (inevitably) that this was a secret code indicating Shakespeare's work on the translation.

Where did we get the idea of the Circles of Hell?

Not from the Bible, that's for sure.

Dante Alighieri, the great Italian writer, composed *The Divine Comedy* between 1308 and 1321. An allegory of the soul's journey toward God, it is divided into three parts: *Inferno*(Hell), *Purgatorio*, and *Paradiso*. Dante's guide in both the Inferno and the Purgatorio is the Roman poet Virgil. In the Inferno, Virgil guides him through the nine circles of Hell, in which they observe sinners suffering punishments that symbolically match their sins.

Seen as one of the glories of Italian literature, *The Divine Comedy* had immense influence for centuries before falling out of favour during the Enlightenment. In the English-speaking world, it was resurrected (so to speak) by the Romantic writers of the late eighteenth and early nineteenth centuries. William Blake, another visionary, illustrated several passages. Henry Wadsworth Longfellow did the first U.S. translation in 1867. Among other translators was Dorothy Sayers, author of the Lord Peter Wimsey mysteries. Many authors have drawn on it for inspiration, including T.S. Eliot, Ezra Pound, Samuel Beckett, C.S. Lewis, and James Joyce.

Today it is hard to remember that the Circles of Hell are not from the Bible.

Where did we get the idea that Satan was a fallen angel?

The title of John Milton's *Paradise Lost* puts us in the picture. This is a work that retells the story of the Fall of Adam and Eve, their expulsion from the Garden of Eden, and the introduction of sin and suffering into the world. Milton also planned to explore the relationship of God to His creation, as Milton himself put it, "to justify the ways of God to men."

In Milton's epic poem written in blank verse (published 1667), Satan, or Lucifer, is a central character. He and some of his fellow angels have been cast into Hell for their rebellious attempt to seize Heaven from God. However, Satan is not repentant. He utters the famous line, "Better to reign in Hell than serve in Heaven." He then volunteers to go to Earth as a spoiler to introduce sin. Assuming the body of a snake, he talks Eve into eating the fruit of the Tree of Knowledge of Good and Evil, and the rest, as they say, is history.

Paradise Lost is considered one of English literature's crowning achievements. John Dryden, no insignificant writer himself, compared Milton to Homer and Virgil. Samuel Johnson was also a fan, though he said of the multi-volume, multi-line work, "None ever wished it longer than it is." It has been quoted by writers ever since, and illustrated frequently by artists such as William Blake and Gustave Doré.

Although the idea of Satan as a fallen angel had existed before, this is when it really took hold.

Quickies
Did you know ...
• that Milton was blind when he wrote *Paradise Lost*. He dictated the work to a series of aides.

What is the official "epic novel" of Massachusetts?

On October 9, 2008, the Massachusetts House of Representatives passed a bill that named Herman Melville's *Moby-Dick* as the state's "official epic novel."

This book, written in 1851, also contains a great deal of allegory, including biblical allegory. The mysterious white whale that wreaks havoc unexpectedly, rising from the depths of the ocean to do so, is often seen as symbolizing fate or the things in life that are out of the control of human beings.

Captain Ahab, the driven captain of the whaling boat is clearly named after the wicked King Ahab in the Bible, who followed false gods. In his single-minded obsession with the pursuit of the whale Moby-Dick, and his determination to have revenge on Moby-Dick for the loss of his leg, he brings death and destruction on everyone and everything around him.

The narrator, Ishmael, a lonely outsider who is the sole survivor of Ahab's crew, is named after Ishmael, Abraham's son by the slave Hagar. When Isaac, the son of Abraham and his wife, Sarah, is born, Sarah has Hagar and Ishmael banished into the desert. Thus the name has come to stand for orphans and exiles.

There is also, of course, the parallel with Jonah and the whale in the book of Jonah.

In his later novel Billy Budd (found unfinished among Melville's papers and published in 1924), Melville, in his use of language, takes great pains to identify the sunny-natured and innocent Billy as a Christ figure. The 1962 movie, directed by Peter Ustinov, starred a young and dewy Terence Stamp as Billy Budd.

Quickies
Did you know ...
- that the (1956) film adaptation of *Moby-Dick* starred Gregory Peck as Captain Ahab. Director John Huston had intended to cast his grizzled father Walter Huston in the role, but Huston Senior had died.
- The movie poster carried the blazing headline "Before the Shark, there was the Whale."

What are the four biblical films that have made it into the top hundred highest-grossing films in the United States and Canada — adjusted for inflation?

The four films are: *The Ten Commandments* (1956) at #4; *Ben-Hur* (1959) at #13; *The Robe* (1953) at #44; and *The Passion of the Christ* (2004) at #57.

The Ten Commandments (1956)
— estimated tickets sold, 131,000,000; $996,910,000 adjusted gross.

This retelling of the story of Moses was Cecil B. DeMille's final film before ill health forced him to give up directing. In fact, it is partly a remake of DeMille's 1923 film of the same name (although the earlier film was only half biblical; the other half was a morality tale that was set in modern times), and some of the cast and crew of the 1923 version were "recycled" in the 1956 version.

The film starred Charlton Heston as Moses, and legend has it that DeMille chose Heston for the role because he thought Heston resembled Michelangelo's famous statue of Moses (without the horns, that is). Heston, in turn, was a great admirer of DeMille, who had directed him in *The Greatest Show on Earth* (1952). As he said, "If you can't make a career out of two DeMille's, you'll never do it."

Yul Brynner was Pharoah (identified in the film as Ramses II, almost certainly inaccurately); Anne Baxter was Mrs. Pharaoh, Nefretiri; Edward G. Robinson was bad guy Dathan. Others in the cast were Yvonne de Carlo, John Derek, Sir Cedric Hardwicke (as Yul Brynner's father), Nina Foch, and Vincent Price. Labouring in bit parts were unknowns Herb Alpert and Robert Vaughan. Heston's newborn son, Fraser, did a float-on as the infant Moses (and reportedly, a diaper pin also made an appearance).

DeMille and his committee of writers did extensive historical research, supplementing biblical accounts with the Koran, which includes details that are left out of Bible, and the writings of Josephus. One interesting coincidence was that the robe striped with white, black, and rust that was worn by Moses was designed to be impressive. Only later was it discovered that these were the actual colours of Moses' tribe, the Tribe of Levi.

The film won an Oscar for its visual effects. One of these was the parting of the Red Sea, which was actually arrived at by filming water pouring from tanks on the back lot, and then running the film in reverse. In the 1923 version of the *Ten Commandments*, the same scene had been created by slicing a slab of Jell-O in two and filming the quivering mass in close-up. Combined with a shot of the Israelites walking into the distance, this proved very effective.

The Library of Congress selected the film to be preserved in the United States National Film Registry in 1999, citing its significance "culturally, historically, or aesthetically." In June 2008, the American Film Institute acknowledged it as the tenth best film in the epic genre.

The fact that it treats biblical accuracy rather offhandedly has never dimmed its popularity. And as Charlton Heston said, "There's a special excitement in playing a man who made a hole in history large enough to be remembered centuries after he died."

Ben-Hur (1959)
— estimated tickets sold, 98,000,000; $745,780,000 adjusted gross.

Based on an 1880 novel by Lew Wallace entitled *Ben-Hur: A Tale of the Christ*, this movie was the top-grossing film of 1960, and went on to win eleven Academy Awards, including Best Picture, Best Leading Actor for Charlton Heston, Best Supporting Actor for Hugh Griffith, and Best Director for William Wyler.

The story — which could be referred to as extra-biblical — concerns a prominent Jerusalem merchant named Judah Ben-Hur. When a childhood friend Messala, now a Roman tribune, is made captain of the garrison in Jerusalem, he tries to use their previous relationship to convince Ben-Hur to inform on Jews who are against the Roman government. When Ben-Hur refuses, the friendship turns to enmity, and Messala uses an unfortunate accident to get Ben-Hur sentenced to be a galley slave. As the slaves are marching to the sea, Ben-Hur collapses from thirst in Nazareth, and Jesus, a local carpenter, gives him water and encourages him on his way.

Several years pass in the galleys, and then Ben-Hur ends up on the flagship of a Roman consul, Quintus Arrius, who recognizes his sterling qualities and gives him more freedom. This is just as well, because in a battle with pirates Ben-Hur is able to save the day and Arrius' life. The grateful Arrius adopts him. With wealth and status as a Roman citizen Ben-Hur returns to Judea to find that Messala is to be a competitor in an upcoming chariot race. Burning with a desire for revenge, Ben-Hur enters the race and wins. Messala, in attempting to sabotage Ben-Hur is fatally injured.

Ben-Hur finds his mother and sister who are now lepers, but his love interest, Esther, has heard Jesus speak and suggests they approach him. Unfortunately, Jesus' trial has started, and they can't get close. It is only as Jesus is on the way to crucifixion that Ben-Hur recognizes him as the carpenter who helped him so many years before, and he attempts to return the favour by offering Jesus water. After he witnesses the crucifixion Ben-Hur is healed of his bitterness, and his mother and sister are literally healed — by a miracle.

Throughout the movie, the face of Jesus is rarely shown, which was in keeping with the wishes of the original author, Lew Wallace. On the publication of the book in 1880, he resisted many requests to have the book dramatized, because he objected to any portrayal of Christ on stage. It was not until dramatist William Young came up with the idea of representing Christ by a beam of light that Wallace would agree. This is what Young did in the stage adaptation of 1899, and the show went on to run for twenty-one years. (In the 1959 movie, the role was actually played by opera singer Claude Heater, who did not get a credit for the part.)

Charlton Heston was not the first choice for the role of Judah Ben-Hur. Burt Lancaster, Rock Hudson, and Canada's own Leslie Nielson turned it down. So did Paul Newman, who said he didn't have the legs to wear a tunic. In the 1925 film version, Ben-Hur had been played by silent-film star Ramon Novarro.

As a massive spectacular, the movie presented many problems in filming. The galley scene was shot indoors, and first the boat had to be cut in half to allow room for the cameras, then the oars had to be shortened, then they had to be weighted to make the rowing of the slaves look sufficiently difficult.

The chariot scene is legendary in movie history. Filmed outside Rome, it took three months and used 15,000 extras. Charlton Heston even spent four weeks taking chariot-driving lessons. Although there was a persistent rumour that a stuntman was killed during the filming of the sequence, William Wyler always strongly denied it. He also mentioned that no horses were injured, in contrast to the 1925 version, in which several horses were killed.

In 2008, the American Film Institute named Ben-Hur as the number-two spot in its list of Top Ten Epics.

The Robe (1953)
— estimated tickets sold, 65,454,500; $498,109,100 adjusted gross.

Based on Lloyd C. Douglas's best-selling 1942 novel of the same name, this film tells the story of the (fictional) Roman tribune Marcellus Gallio, who was in charge of the crucifixion of Jesus. He and some soldiers cast dice for Jesus' robe, and Marcellus wins. However, when he is caught in a rainstorm and orders his servant to throw the robe over him, Marcellus has an excruciating seizure and begins to regret the crucifixion of Jesus, a feeling that he suppresses. The servant runs off with the robe, and Marcellus is ordered by the Emperor Tiberius to find the robe and destroy it — oh yes, and to identify the followers of Jesus so they can be arrested. Marcellus sets out on his mission eagerly, but through the intervention of Peter the apostle and his own experiences with the Robe, Marcellus is converted to Christianity. This does not go down well with Rome, and Marcellus is arrested by Caligula (the fiancé of Marcellus's love interest, Diana). Since he will not renounce Christ, Marcellus is condemned to death, and Diana joins him.

Lloyd C. Douglas was an immensely popular author from the 1930s to the 1960s, though he hadn't start to write until he retired from the ministry in mid-life (an American, he was serving in a church in Montreal at the time of his retirement). The book was inspired by a letter from one of his fans, who wrote to ask Douglas what he thought had happened to Christ's garments after his death. Matthew 27:35 reads, "And they crucified him and parted his garments, casting lots," and the other gospels all mention the same detail. This was enough to fire Douglas's imagination, and *The Robe* was the result.

The film starred Richard Burton as Marcellus and Jean Simmons as his beloved Diana. Victor Mature played the slave/servant Demetrius who is instrumental in the plot, while Pontius Pilate was played by Richard Boone, who went on to fame on television as the gunfighter Paladin in *Have Gun — Will Travel* (1957–63). Rumour has it that Richard Burton hated the movie so much that he refused a contract with 20th Century Fox. This dislike was possibly reflected in his performance, which was described at the time as "wooden." Even he was astonished when he received an Oscar nomination.

Historical accuracy suffered in the film. Caligula was portrayed as the persecutor of Christians, but Roman persecution of the early church really got under way under Nero.

The Robe was the only biblical epic that had a sequel. It was followed a year later, by *Demetrius and the Gladiators* (1954), starring Victor Mature.

The Passion of the Christ (2004)
— estimated tickets sold, 59,704,800; $454, 354,353,800.

This movie begins with Jesus praying in the Garden of Gethsemane just before he is betrayed and ends with his resurrection.

The production was directed, co-produced, and co-written by Mel Gibson, and is based almost totally on the four gospels of Matthew, Mark, Luke, and John. Gibson and his company Icon Productions also totally funded the production costs of some $30 million and the marketing costs of around $15 million, because Gibson could not find anyone else who would take it on.

To the astonishment of many, Gibson decided to film the movie in Latin and Aramaic, with subtitles. He and his co-writer Benedict Fitzgerald wrote the script in English, and then Friar William Fulco SJ translated it into Latin, Hebrew, and reconstructed Aramaic. Friar Fulco, a professor of ancient Mediterranean studies at Loyola Marymount University, also served as the religious consultant on the film. *The Passion of the Christ* became the highest-grossing non-English language film ever.

Reactions to the film were mixed, even among believers. Some worried that the film was anti-Semitic, others that it contained historical inaccuracies. Some were intensely moved while others felt that Gibson dwelt to a suspicious extent on the very extreme violence (in fact, the movie got an R rating because of the violence). One upset viewer summed up the latter reaction by referring to "this steak-tartare Christ." Gibson acknowledged the violence, saying that he intended to portray the enormity of what Christ suffered.

Quickies

Did you know ...

- that during filming of *The Passion of the Christ*, assistant director Jan Michelini was struck by lightning twice. As the BBC reported on October 23, 2003, the second strike also hit the actor playing Jesus, James Caviezel. Hmmm.

Which successful musical portrays Judas as a sympathetic figure?

Jesus Christ Superstar, by Tim Rice and Andrew Lloyd Webber, was released first as an album, and many feel this was the definitive version of the rock musical.

On October 12, 1971, it opened on Broadway to mixed reviews, though it was to win Andrew Lloyd Webber a 1972 Tony Award for Best Original Score. The same year, Ben Vereen, who played Judas, won both a Theatre World Award and a Tony for Best Featured Actor.

It seems somehow fitting that the actor who played Judas was singled out for attention, since the Webber/Rice script takes an unconventional approach, doing a renovation job on the character of Judas.

The action covers the events of the story of Christ from the approach to Jerusalem to the crucifixion. At every juncture, Judas is portrayed as an earnest man who is deeply concerned that Jesus is (as he sees it) out of control and determined to bring down the wrath of Rome on his followers. He is disturbed that more and more people are hailing Jesus' as a king, and warns Jesus to tone it down.

An exhausted Jesus is given an oil massage by the prostitute Mary Magdalene, who is in love with him. Judas objects both to Jesus' association with a sinner, which could bring condemnation on their work, and to the waste of the money spent on the ointment, which could have been given to the poor. This, of course, uses the common perception of Mary Magdalene as a "fallen woman," which is nowhere supported in the Bible (along with her identification with the woman with the ointment), and transforms an act of repentance and devotion into something quite different. Judas does voice some objection to the money "wasted" on the ointment in the Bible, but many commentators feel that, as the treasurer of the group, Judas was more concerned with getting the money into his own hands.

Judas's final betrayal of Jesus is meant to keep him from bringing suffering on the people by drawing down punishment from Rome. The priests also point out that the twenty pieces of silver can be given to charity.

After Jesus is treated harshly by the authorities, Judas regrets his actions. He finally commits suicide, and the dying Jesus sees his spirit, which is saying, in effect, "Was this really necessary?"

Webber and Rice were quite open about the fact that they didn't see Jesus as God, and their portrayal of a very human Jesus grows out of that. As so often happens in any treatment of a religious theme, some members of almost every faith found reason to be offended. Some Jewish groups felt the musical was anti-Semitic, while some Christian groups thought it was blasphemous.

The public loved it.

Which movie portrays Keanu Reeves
as a Christ figure?

In *The Matrix* (1999), Keanu Reeves is Thomas Anderson, a computer pro-
grammer who moonlights as a hacker named "Neo." His search for the
origins of something called the Matrix connect him with a rebel group
led by an underground hacker named "Morpheus" (Lawrence Fishburne).
Morpheus and the rebels show him that what he thought was the world is a
simulated reality called the Matrix, created by intelligent machines to keep
humans docile while they harvest their body heat and electrical energy.
The rebels are freed human beings. They help Neo break free and take him
to the rebel headquarters, where Morpheus tells Neo that he believes Neo
is "the One" who will fulfil a prophecy. The One is said to be a man who
will finally defeat the machines and save the humans.

The rest of the movie records the struggle of Neo, which is an anagram
for One, and the rebels to defeat the machines and the Matrix and save
humanity.

Although the film cites many influences, the Christian symbolism is
clear. Even the name of Reeves's character is telling. The name "Thomas"
recalls "Doubting Thomas" in the Bible and is fitting for a man who doubts
his own mission. The name "Anderson" translates as "son of man," which is
the term applied to Jesus in the Bible. It links Jesus to the promised Messiah
who will "save humanity."

The details pile on. The rebel base is called "Zion," the name of the
hill on which Jerusalem is built. Morpheus can also be seen to parallel
John the Baptist, who announced that Jesus was "the Anointed One."
Neo dies, but he is brought back to life by the love of Trinity. Need we
go on?

Just to nail it down, a character early in the film says: "You're my
saviour, man."

question
and feature list

The Book

What does the name *Bible* mean?, 14
What is the Hebrew Bible?, 14
Who first collected the books of the Old Testament?, 14
When was the Bible first translated?, 15
How many passages do some claim were written by God?, 15
How many versions of the Bible are there in English?, 15
When was the Bible first translated into English?, 15
Which Bible did Shakespeare use?, 16
Quickies, 16
When was the King James Bible published?, 17
The Books of the Bible, 17
What is the Apocrypha?, 18
How many books are there in the Protestant Bible?, 18
Quickies, 18
What did Voltaire get wrong?, 18
How many Bibles are distributed in the United States every day?, 19
The Apocrypha, 19
What is *bibliomancy*?, 19
Bible Stats, 20
What was the first major book printed with movable type?, 20
What is the most expensive modern Bible?, 21
What is the largest printed Bible?, 21
What is the world's smallest Bible?, 21
Bibles with Errors, 23

Genesis:
The Beginnings

What was the order in which God created the elements of the earth?, 28
Ten longest names in the Bible, 28
What does the name *Adam* mean?, 28
What does the name *Eve* mean?, 29

How did God create a woman out of Adam's rib and do men have fewer ribs?, 29

Adam's Rib, 29

How does "Adam's rib" relate to relations between the sexes?, 29

Why was the fruit that Adam and Eve ate an apple?, 30

Where did the term *Adam's apple* come from?, 30

Why did God plant the tree in the Garden of Eden if he didn't want Adam and Eve to eat the fruit?, 30

Where do we get the term *forbidden fruit*?, 30

What other trees were in the Garden of Eden?, 31

Why do snakes slither, according to the Bible?, 31

What is the first incident of sibling rivalry in the Bible?, 31

What is the Mark of Cain?, 32

Am I My Brother's Keeper?, 32

The Mark of Cain, 32

Who founded the first city?, 32

Quickies, 32

How is the Land of Nod associated with children's nursery rhymes?, 33

How many children did Adam and Eve have?, 33

Who is the oldest man recorded in the Bible?, 33

What kind of boat is an ark?, 33

How large was the Ark in the Bible?, 34

How many of each living thing did Noah take with him on the Ark?, 34

How long were Noah and his family on the Ark?, 34

Quickies, 35

Where did the Ark "land"?, 35

Why is the dove with an olive branch in its beak a symbol of peace?, 35

Quickies, 35

Why does the word *babble* refer to "confused or incoherent" speech?, 36

Quickies, 36

What is *tithing,* and where did it come from?, 36

Where did the practice of circumcision come from?, 36

Why are the cities of Sodom and Gomorrah a symbol of sin and loose living?, 37

Lot's Wife, 37

Why do we say someone has "sold their birthright for a mess of pottage"?, 38

Why is the flexible ladder on a ship, which allows people to climb up to the deck from a small boat, called a *Jacob's ladder*?, 38

Quickies, 39

What colour was Joseph's coat — really?, 39

Where did we get the expression "Living off the fat of the land"?, 39

The Books of Moses:
Exodus, Leviticus, Numbers, and Deuteronomy

Why did the Egyptian king (Pharaoh) order all newborn male babies born to the Israelites to be thrown into the Nile River?, 41

What does the name *Moses* mean?, 41

Who wrote the song "Oh! Let My People Go"?, 42

Which Pharaoh is it that "lets the people go"?, 42

Where did the expression "Bricks with no straw" come from?, 43

What failing does Moses claim in order to get out of the task of confronting Pharaoh?, 43

Quickies, 43

What are the plagues that God inflicts on Egypt?, 44

What is the origin of Passover?, 44

Quickies, 45

How long were the Israelites in Egypt?, 45

How many Israelites left Egypt?, 45

What is the body of water the Israelites cross to finally escape from Pharaoh's pursuit?, 45

What is manna?, 46

Top 10 most mentioned animals, 46

Quickies, 47

Where did the word *fleshpots* come from?, 47

Why did Moses break the first two stone tablets containing the Ten Commandments?, 47

Quickies, 48

What is the order of the Ten Commandments?, 48

Why does Michelangelo's famous statue of Moses have horns?, 49

The Wicked Bible, 49

Quickies, 49

What was the Ark of the Covenant?, 49

Quickies, 50

How did the book of Leviticus get its name?, 50

What is a scapegoat?, 50

Indiana Jones and the Ark of the Covenant, 51

What is kosher?, 51

Quickies, 52

Why do we say, "An eye for an eye and tooth for a tooth"?, 52

Who had the longest bed in the Bible?, 53

Why do the logos of many medical organizations use a snake curled around a rod?, 53

What does the name *Deuteronomy* mean?, 54

Quickies, 54

Where is Moses buried and who buried him?, 54

Getting Settled:
The Books of Samuel, Kings,and Chronicles

What do the judges Samuel and Samson have in common?, 56

What was King Saul's most noticeable physical characteristic?, 56

What do we mean by "a man after one's own heart"?, 56

What was David's special talent?, 56

What do we mean by a "David and Goliath" contest?, 57

Quickies, 57

Quickies, 57

How did Saul's children save David's life?, 58

Quickies, 58

Who is the Witch of Endor?, 59

Quickies, 59

Quickies, 60

Where do we get the expression "How are the mighty fallen"?, 60

Top 10 most common nouns in the Bible, 60

When did Jerusalem become the capital of Israel?, 60

Who was the original heir to David's throne?, 61

Quickies, 61

Who is Zadok the Priest, and why did Handel write an anthem about him?, 61

Absalom and Literature, 62

Quickies, 63

Quickies, 63

Why is a wise person referred to as a "Solomon"?, 63

How many wives did Solomon have?, 64

When did Solomon build the Temple in Jerusalem?, 64

Was Solomon married to the Queen of Sheba?, 64

The Queen of Sheba in Film, 65

Quickies, 66

Why is a very large bottle of wine called a "Jeroboam"?, 66

Why is a wicked woman referred to as a "Jezebel"?, 67

Who was the fastest sprinter in the Bible?, 68

Why is a reckless driver known as a "Jehu"?, 68

Who was taken up to heaven in a fiery chariot?, 69

"Swing Low, Sweet Chariot", 69

Who is the grouchiest bald man in the Bible?, 70

Who had the longest reign of any king of Judah or Israel?, 70

When are the city of Jerusalem and the Temple destroyed and when does the Babylonian captivity begin?, 70

Judges and Priests: Joshua, Judges, and Ruth

Who was the prostitute who helped the Israelites to conquer the Promised Land?, 72

Why has crossing the Jordan River become associated with dying?, 72

Joshua Fit de Battle of Jericho, 73

Who did the Israelites finally bury in the Promised Land?, 73

What is meant by *judges* in the Book of Judges?, 74

Top 10 longest-lived people in the bible, 74

Who is the only left-handed person mentioned in the Bible?, 74

Who is the first woman to lead the Israelites?, 75

Who is the woman that Deborah credits with aiding the Israelite victory
    over the Canaanites?, 75

Why did Samson not cut his hair?, 76

The Gideon Bible, 76

Samson and Delilah (1949), 77

What is the first riddle in the Bible?, 77

Quickies, 78

Who is descended from Ruth and Boas, her second husband?, 78

What does footwear have to do with giving a pledge?, 78

Ruth, Henry VIII, and Levirate Marriage, 79

Prophets, Major and Minor

What does the word *prophet* mean?, 81

Were there women prophets?, 81

How are the words of the prophet Isaiah represented at the United
    Nations headquarters in New York?, 82

What is a plowshare?, 82

Isaiah and Handel's Messiah, 82

Where do we get the expression "Holier than thou"?, 83

What does the name *Immanuel* mean?, 83

Does the word *virgin* in the Bible refer to ... well, a virgin?, 83

Where do we get the expression "A lamb to the slaughter"?, 83

Who is the Bible's first nudist?, 84

Where did we get the expression "No rest for the wicked"?, 84

What do we mean by "put your house in order"?, 85

How does Isaiah die?, 85

Where do we get the expression "A drop in the bucket"?, 85

Who is the Bible's most noted depressive?, 85

Why do we ask, "Can a leopard change its spots?", 86

What do we mean by "sour grapes"?, 86
"Dem Dry Bones", 86
Who does God order to marry a prostitute?, 87
What is the shortest book in the Hebrew Bible?, 87
What was it that swallowed Jonah?, 87
Which prophet was instrumental in the magi finding Jesus?, 88

Exile and Homecoming:
Ezra, Nehemiah, Esther, and Daniel

Who are the first in the Bible to choose vegetarianism?, 90
Why do we speak of someone having "feet of clay"?, 90
Who was thrown into the "fiery furnace"?, 91
Where did the expression "The writing is on the wall" come from?, 91
Top 10 occupations in biblical times, 92
Why do we refer to someone facing an intimidating experience as "Daniel in the lions' den"?, 93
Quickies, 94
Daniel, Shakespeare, and Rumpole of the Bailey, 94
What is Esther's connection with Haddassah, the Jewish volunteer women's organization?, 94
What book of the Bible never mentions God?, 96
When was the Second Temple in Jerusalem built?, 96
Quickies, 96

Writings, Poetry, and Songs — Job, Psalms, Proverbs, Ecclesiastes, Song of Songs

What is meant by the word *proverb*?, 98
Who wrote the book of Proverbs?, 98
What does Proverbs have to do with the Humane Society?, 98
Where do we get the expression "Pride goes before a fall"?, 98
Where does it say, "Spare the rod and spoil the child"?, 99

What does the name Satan mean?, 99

Quickies, 99

What is meant by a "Job's comforter"?, 99

Quickies, 100

Where do we get the expression "By the skin of your teeth"?, 100

What does the word *vanity* mean in Ecclesiastes?, 100

Where do we get the expression "Nothing new under the sun"?, 101

Where does it say, "Eat, drink, and be merry"?, 101

Quickies, 101

Where do we get the expression "A fly in the ointment"?, 101

To Every Thing There Is a Season, 102

What is the advice Ecclesiastes gives to publishers?, 102

Top 10 most mentioned names, 102

Why is the "Song of Songs" also called the "Song of Solomon"?, 102

Quickies, 103

What is an orphaned psalm?, 103

Where do we get the expression "The apple of my eye"?, 103

What Psalm did Jesus quote on the cross?, 103

Where do we get the expression "From strength to strength"?, 104

What were the most common instruments used in the Bible?, 104

Which psalm inspired Martin Luther's famous hymn "A Mighty Fortress Is Our God"?, 104

Where do we get the expression "At one's wits' end"?, 105

By the Rivers of Babylon, 105

The Life of Jesus — Matthew, Mark, Luke, and John

Did Matthew, Mark, Luke, and John actually write the gospels?, 110

Did Matthew, Mark, Luke, and John know Jesus personally?, 110

What are the symbols of Matthew, Mark, Luke, and John?, 110

What does the word *gospel* mean?, 111

Godspell, 111

Who is the famous ancestor of Mary and Joseph?, 111

Where do the names *Messiah* and *Christ* come from?, 112

Was Jesus really born in a cattle shed?, 112

Quickies, 112

Quickies, 113

What year was Jesus born?, 113

Was Jesus actually born on December 25?, 113

Quickies, 114

Who were the three wise men?, 114

Why did King Herod have mother-in-law issues?, 115

Quickies, 115

Quickies, 115

We Three Kings of Orient Are, 115

What is Jesus's relationship to John the Baptist?, 115

What did John the Baptist eat?, 116

Where do we get the expression "Separate the wheat from the chaff"?, 116

Does John the Baptist have anything to do with the Baptist church?, 116

How did John the Baptist die?, 117

How many days does Jesus spend in the desert before starting his ministry?, 117

Salome, 118

What is the origin of the saying "Get thee behind me, Satan"?, 119

What are the three temptations that Satan offers Jesus?, 119

How old was Jesus when he began his teaching?, 120

What was Jesus's first miracle, and who asked him to perform it?, 120

Where do we get the expression "Physician, heal thyself"?, 120

What was the significance of Jesus choosing twelve followers for his inner circle?, 121

What is the difference between a disciple and an apostle?, 121

Top 10 trees mentioned in the Bible, 122

What are the names of the twelve apostles?, 123

Apostle Spoons, 123

How many of the Apostles were fishermen?, 124

Why has the fish become a symbol of Christianity?, 124

Quickies, 124

Which of the Apostles was a tax collector?, 125

What name does Jesus give to Peter?, 125

Why is Peter pictured as the gatekeeper of Heaven?, 125

What nickname does Jesus give the brothers James and John?, 126

What bird is named after Peter?, 126

Why do we talk about "hiding one's light under a bushel"?, 126

Where do we get the expression "Straight and narrow"?, 127

Quickies, 127

Where did we get the expression "The blind leading the blind"?, 127

Which of the disciples had a "stage mother"?, 127

The Jefferson Bible, 128

Where do we get the expression "Pearls before swine"?, 128

Why do we talk about a "wolf in sheep's clothing"?, 129

How many demons did Christ cast out of Mary Magdalene?, 129

Where did the idea that Mary Magdalene and Jesus were married come from?, 129

Where do we get the expression "A whited sepulchre"?, 130

Quickies, 130

Why are the Beatitudes called the Beatitudes ?, 130

Quickies, 130

Quickies, 130

Where do we get the expression "Salt of the earth"?, 130

Where do we get the expression "A Good Samaritan"?, 131

Where do we get the expression "Go the extra mile"?, 132

What well-known hymn was inspired by the parable of the Prodigal Son?, 132

Amazing Grace, 133

Where do we get the expression "Practise what you preach"?, 134

Who anointed Jesus's feet with ointment?, 134

Quickies, 135

Quickies, 136

What is the significance of Jesus riding into Jerusalem on a donkey?, 136

Why do the people wave palm branches when Jesus enters Jerusalem?, 136

What is a "mite" in the story of the widow's mite?, 136

Where do we get the expression "The left hand doesn't know what the right hand is doing"?, 137

What event does Jesus predict?, 137

Thomas B. Costain: Canada's Author of the Grail, 138

Where do we get the expression "To take someone under your wing"?, 138

What occasion are Jesus and his disciples celebrating at the Last Supper?, 138

Why is the number thirteen considered unlucky in some Christian traditions?, 139

Where do we get the term Eucharist, 139

What is Maundy Thursday?, 139

The Last Supper by Leonardo da Vinci, 140

How much is Judas paid for betraying Christ?, 141

What does the name Gethsemane mean?, 141

Why do we say, "Many are called, but few are chosen"?, 141

Where do we get the expression "The spirit is willing, but the flesh is weak"?, 142

Is it possible to sweat blood?, 142

What act of violence does Peter perform when the soldiers come to arrest Christ?, 143

Where do we get the expression "Turn the other cheek"?, 143

Who was the first "streaker"?, 143

Where do we get the expression "To wash one's hands of something"?, 143

Quickies, 144

Where do we get the expression "Give up the ghost"?, 144

Quickies, 144

Where does the name Easter come from, and why the bunnies and eggs?, 145

Top 10 "bad" women of the Bible, 145

Why is it significant that Jesus appears first to a woman, Mary Magdalene?, 147

Why is the disciple Thomas referred to as Doubting Thomas?, 147

How long does Jesus remain on earth after his resurrection?, 147

The Early Church:
Acts, Romans, Letters to the Churches, and Revelation

Where did Christ ascend to Heaven?, 150

Who replaced Judas Iscariot as the twelfth apostle?, 150

What is considered the birthday of the Christian church?, 150

Quickies, 151

What does *Pentecost* mean?, 151

Who is Gamaliel?, 151

Who was the first Christian martyr?, 152

What future church leader witnesses the death of the first martyr?, 153

Why do we speak of a "Damascus experience"?, 153

When does Saul become Paul?, 154

When was the name *Christian* first used?, 154

Who was the first of the twelve apostles to be martyred?, 154

Where do we get the expression "The powers that be"?, 154

Quickies, 155

What Happened to the Twelve Apostles?, 155

What do we mean by "As you sow, so shall you reap"?, 157

Where do we get the expression "All things to all men"?, 157

Where did the idea of celibacy for priests begin?, 157

Where do we get the expression "A thorn in the flesh"?, 158

Where do we get the word *bishop*?, 158

Quickies, 158

Where do we get the expression "The love of money is the root of all
    evil"?, 158

Where do we get the expression "Fight the good fight"?, 159

What are the Four Horsemen of the Apocalypse?, 159

Quickies, 159

Top 10 misconceptions about the Bible, 160

What city is symbolized by the Great Whore?, 160

What is the Mark of the Beast?, 161

"The Battle Hymn of the Republic", 161

The Bible and Culture

How did Shakespeare use the Bible?, 163
Quickies, 163
Quickies, 164
Where did we get the idea of the Circles of Hell?, 164
Where did we get the idea that Satan was a fallen angel?, 165
Quickies, 165
What is the official "epic novel" of Massachusetts?, 166
Quickies, 166
What are the four biblical films that have made it into the top hundred
    highest-grossing films in the United States and Canada — adjusted
    for inflation?, 167
Quickies, 170
Quickies, 172
Which successful musical portrays Judas as a sympathetic figure?, 172
Which movie portrays Keanu Reeves as a Christ figure?, 174

Other Books in the Now You Know Series

**Now You Know
Big Book of Sports**
978-1-55488-454-4
$29.99

**Now You Know
Royalty**
978-1-55488-415-5
$19.99

**Now You Know
Baseball**
978-1-55488-713-2
$19.99

**Now You Know Big
Book of Answers 2**
978-1-55002-871-3
$29.99

**Now You Know
Hockey**
978-1-55002-869-0
$19.99

**Now You Know
Soccer**
978-1-55488-416-2
$19.99

More Books in the Now You Know Series

Now You Know Golf 978-1-55002-870-6 $19.99
Now You Know Canada's Heroes 978-1-55488-444-5 $19.99
Now You Know Big Book of Answers 978-1-55002-741-9 $29.99
Now You Know Disasters 978-1-55002-807-2 $9.99
Now You Know Pirates 978-1-55002-806-5 $9.99
Now You Know Extreme Weather 978-1-55002-743-3 $9.99
Now You Know Christmas 978-1-55002-745-7 $9.99
Now You Know Crime Scenes 978-1-55002-774-7 $9.99
Now You Know 978-1-55002-461-6 $19.99
Now You Know More 978-1-55002-530-9 $19.99
Now You Know Almost Everything 978-1-55002-575-0 $19.99
Now You Know Volume 4 978-1-55002-648-1 $19.99

Available at your favourite bookseller.

DUNDURN PRESS
www.dundurn.com